John Pilgrim and Ernie Almond

"THE VERY BEST OUT & ABOUT BOOK"

WITH

JOHN PILGRIM

WRITTEN BY JOHN PILGRIM

PHOTOGRAPHY BY DAVID SPAIN

CARTOONS BY NICK MILSTEAD

PRINTED AND PUBLISHED IN 2001
BY ALPINE PRESS

ALPINE PRESS LIMITED
STATION ROAD
KINGS LANGLEY
HERTFORDSHIRE
WD4 8LF

TEL: 01923 269777

ISBN: 0-9528631-4-6

ACKNOWLEDGMENTS

My thanks to Mark Norman, Managing Editor of BBC Three Counties Radio. This is my third book and I am pleased to say that, after initial costs, one pound from each copy sold will be donated directly to BBC Children in Need. In fact a donation was made from the receipts of the first two books to this worthy cause and I thank Mark for his continued support. BBC Local Radio is often forgotten when the plaudits are handed out, we should celebrate the work that our local stations do day in, day out, both in promoting local issues, history and community as well as supporting national causes. We like to think that we are at the forefront when it comes to all that is best in our local community and Mark Norman has shown his dedication to that cause. Thank you Mark, may we break all records with this third book so that Children in Need can continue to be a successful part of our daily life. Let us not forget that BBC Three Counties Radio broke all records at the 2001 Sony Radio Awards, Jon Gaunt won three gold awards a feat never before achieved in the same year and Stephen Rhodes Consumer Programme followed other award winning performances with a Gold Award. Having congratulated and thanked the BBC! It is my privilege to meet directly the people of Beds, Herts, Bucks and beyond, to them I say a big thank you, without your contributions to the radio programme these books would not be possible. Local historians, writers and various other experts contribute on a daily basis.

THANK YOU ONE AND ALL!

THANKS TO:

BBC Three Counties Radio, Hazel Acus, Ernie Almond, Larry Adler, Elkie Brookes, June Brown, Barry the Boiler, Bedford Tourist Office, John Brindle, Phil Bridle, Bedford Borough Council, Bekonscot Model Village, Martin Baggot, Jack Bromfield and the members of BARG, Vic Botterill, Bucks Railway Centre at Quainton, Richard Casserley, Sebastian Coe, John Cooke, Francis Cory-Wright, Bill Collins, Martyn Coote, Paul Daniels, Eric Evans, Nigel Gayler, Andrew Green, Bill Griffiths, Phil Gooden, Jon and Lisa Gaunt, Bethany and Rosie, Alan Goldsmith, Gloria Hunniford, William Hague, Roy Hudd, Half Man / Half Mac, Maureen Hird, Hardware Café in Luton, Ken Haughton, John and Bill Jordan, Kodak Ltd., Lynn in Denham, Sir Patrick Moore, Buster Merryfield, Mark Norman, Jane Oakley, June O' Mahoney, Peter Page, Jenny Pates, Michael Portillo, James Perry, Roberto Perrone, Bill Pilgrim, George Pilgrim, Ollie Phillips and the Watford Observer, The RAF Museum at Hendon, Jon Richardson, Charlie Ross, John Saunders, Sue and Chris Scott, Linda and Paul Seeley, Alice Spain, Fred Stoughton, Dave the Thatch, Ken Thomson, Friends of West Norwood Cemetery, Grelle White, Kevin Whately, Fatima Whitbread, Geoff & Sue Woodward, Donald Wratten.

John and David would like to thank all the staff at Alpine Press who were involved in the production of this book, with thanks to the Repro Department, especially Matthew Barbero and Terry Sartin for their creativity and having to put up with Spainy!

Special Thanks to Chloe Fletcher and Jackie Butchart, David's Assistant Photographers who took the photographs whilst he was snoozing!

TABLE OF CONTENTS

INTRODUCTION

He is large! And I do mean large, no let's face it, he's much more than large, he's, well I can't use the word I would like to, no point in upsetting you at this early stage, overweight is the word to use (in polite circles). He also went to a very posh school, two reasons why I shouldn't have invited D. Spain esquire to make the trips with me. There are other reasons, he has absolutely no dress sense at all and he eats like the proverbial horse. Having got that off my chest, let me explain our mission. A series of journeys across the Counties of Beds, Herts and Bucks. The aim, to discover some of the lesser known historical facts and fictions along the way, visit them, photograph them ('Spainy's' job) and record them. Not an unworthy or tiresome task, that is unless you are accompanied by 'Spainy'. He has, let us say, his little foibles and for my sins I was about to experience some of them for the first time! Read and enjoy.

John Pilgrim, Sandy, Bedfordshire

August 2001

'Spainy' and his telephone box in the front garden of 'Spain Towers'

CHAPTER 1 - BEDFORD AND BREAKFAST

Day one, Bedford town centre, we had agreed to meet at The Swan Hotel situated on the banks of the River Great Ouse. It was my suggestion and I admit it! I wanted our trip to get off to a civilised start and The Swan Hotel is civilised. Our intention was to leave our cars at the railway station in order that we could travel through to Luton by train stopping along the way at places of interest (or in 'Spainys' case, likely looking greasy spoon 'caffs'). So I parked and walked back to the hotel to await my companion. 'Spainy' arrived late, nothing new there then! The tee shirt he was wearing was black, at least it had been at one time, now it was more camouflage. We took our seats in the breakfast room and I made some notes.

There has been an inn on the site of the Swan since 1507; the 17th century saw the building used as chambers for judges. It was to the Swan that the wife of John Bunyan came to plead for her husband's release from jail. She was turned down and her husband sat down to write 'The Pilgrims Progress'. The present building was commissioned by none other than the fifth Duke of Bedford. The Duke wanted to take away the business from The Red Lion because he didn't want anyone else earning the 'dosh' but he spent a lot of cash in pursuit of his wish. It's a fancy place all right, even if they did let 'Spainy' in. The front porch has a balcony resting on four pillars; the Duke purchased a rather elegant staircase from Houghton House (used by Bunyan as the model for his House Beautiful and included in our itinerary). After the railway came to Bedford the Swan maintained its social position in the town and it could be said that it still does, after all it is grand, it stands on a great river and we took breakfast there. Having comfortably cleared the kitchens of sausages, bread, eggs, tomatoes and bacon along with odd cup of tea or three or four, my friend ambled off to take some 'snaps'. I call them 'snaps' - he calls them photographs.

Bedford has a lot to commend it, there again it has a few things that could be improved, the flow of traffic through the town for a start, or to be precise, you could hardly call it a flow, more of a trickle. Best to visit by train I think, unless you are privy to the secrets of 'Park and Ride'. Doubtless the town is best known for its connection with the aforementioned John Bunyan, tinker and writer. You would imagine that, with my surname, I would be able to quote you chapter and verse on the subject of Bunyan, but I can't. I know that he grew up in the nearby village of Elstow, and that he was a pretty ordinary sort of a kid, though perhaps a little rowdy. Bunyan was born in 1660 and at the age of sixteen he joined the Parliamentary forces, and probably spent his military service at nearby Newport Pagnall. His military career is somewhat sketchy but we do know that he returned to Elstow and earned his living as a tinker. At around this time a Royalist by the name of Gifford who had escaped from Maidstone prison arrived in Bedford and set up an Independent church. In 1653 Bunyan cast off his former ways and joined Gifford's church. Bunyan had several brushes with the law but continued with his new found beliefs. Later on and with religion top of his agenda, Bunyan set out for Lower Samsell near Harlington to preach. By this time good old Gifford had passed on and Bunyan had taken on the mantle. He was arrested by the local justice, Francis Wingate, who lived at Harlington Hall. We need not go into the details here, there are several good books on the subject of Mr. Bunyan, sufficient to say that, he and his friends were considered to have broken the law. Bunyan began a twelve year stretch. The erstwhile tinker refused to compromise his beliefs, if he had then he would have been released. But he didn't and instead wrote 'The Pilgrims Progress'. I have to say at this point, that I believe (and it maybe because of my surname) that just about everyone I ever met has heard of John Bunyan and 'The Pilgrims Progress', but I can't think of anyone who admits to ever having read it! Which is a pretty good thing for whoever publishes the book and not for anyone else! Least of all Bunyan, since he is long gone and has no need of the money.

John Bunyan window

Statue of John Howard outside 'Swan Hotel'

There is a statue and museum commemorating Bunyan in Bedford and in front of the 'Swan' hotel is a statue of another worthy Bedfordian John Howard. The seventeen year period starting with Howard's appointment as High Sheriff of Bedfordshire and ending with his death, in Russia in 1790 was, quote *"a period which included several crucial developments in the history of imprisonment."* Howard was a non conformist and a member of the Bunyan Meeting until his appointment as High Sheriff. He was not a Bedfordshire man but he lived locally for many years in the villages of Cardington and Elstow. In Cardington he competed with Sam Whitbread (one of any number of Whitbreads of brewing fame) to improve the lot of the villagers. On becoming High Sheriff, John Howard attended the Assize in Bedford and was disgusted to find that, even though some prisoners were found not guilty, they continued to be imprisoned because they couldn't pay the jailer for their keep! Howard reports these details in his work: *'must pay before discharge, fifteen shillings and fourpence to the jailer, and two shillings to the turnkey. All persons that come to this place either by warrant, commitment or verbally'.* A pretty state of affairs, I think you will agree (though it bears saying that in 'Spainys' case, he could have learned a lesson from this salutary tale and paid half the breakfast bill at The Swan to atone for his earlier misdemeanours). Howard travelled far and wide, particularly in Russia and fought for penal reform. A great and good man was John Howard, his house at Cardington has a wonderful garden (not open to the public), which I have been privileged to visit. All this information was gleaned as I awaited the return of my favourite photographer. Finally he arrived, hot and sweaty and with a rather guilty look, "And where have you been?" I asked, he shifted his feet and looked at them, I can always tell when he is about to tell a 'porkie', "Oh just taking a few snaps." I admonished him in a suitable manner, not suitable to print, and we departed The Swan Hotel. Our walk to the railway station took us past the Corn Exchange where Glenn Miller broadcast his much loved music during World War Two. Miller is remembered in Bedford to this day, and quite rightly so. It is still one of the unsolved mysteries of the war as to just how the bandleader met his end.

It is said (and I cannot say more than that, because my friend Pete Worby has another theory) that Miller left Twinwoods airfield, close to Bedford to fly to Paris for a concert, he never arrived. I have broadcast several programmes from the Corn Exchange and each time I do, someone comes up with another theory as to what happened to Glenn Miller. Pete Worby asks this question, "David Niven (the actor) was in Bedford at the same time as Miller, it was Niven who arranged Miller's lodgings in Bedford. Niven was something very secret during the war and never mentioned his connection with Miller in his two part biography. Pete asks simply why? Pete also claims that the aircraft in which the bandleader is supposed to have met his end, was still on this earth way after the time it was supposed to have disappeared into the great blue yonder. That 'Blue Angel' Marlene Deitrich may well have also been involved; she was a girl friend of actor James Stewart who, coincidentally, played Miller in the film of his life. Pete also tells me that the room where Miller lodged in Bedford was cleared the very next day his disappearance was reported. Another story places Miller in Paris the day after he left England, it goes on to state that an American soldier was shot in the street because of an affair he was having with a married woman. Quite what June Allyson would have thought, I can only guess! (In case you don't know, June played Mrs Miller in the film). 'Spainy' and I continued our ten minute walk to Bedford railway station, as we passed through the Harpur Centre (plenty of shops of all kinds and the occasional busker) my overweight friend happened to mention his visit to the Cecil Higgins Gallery. He has a habit of doing this to me, just when I am about to impart some tiny gem of information, 'Spainy' comes up with something to top it. "Cecil Higgins" he said, "Eliza Doolittle" I said, "No that was Professor Higgins" he replied as he played with his attachments (on his camera, I hasten to add). "OK, so what about Cecil Higgins?"

Bust of Glenn Miller outside Corn Exchange

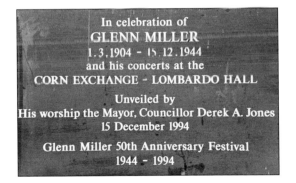

In celebration of
GLENN MILLER
1.3.1904 - 15.12.1944
and his concerts at the
CORN EXCHANGE - LOMBARDO HALL
Unveiled by
His worship the Mayor, Councillor Derek A. Jones
15 December 1994

Glenn Miller 50th Anniversary Festival
1944 - 1994

It seems that Cecil Higgins got off to a rather bad start in life, he hated the 19th century, so (as you would) he decided to do something about it. Nothing earth shattering, you understand, but more than enough to earn the undying gratitude of thousands of Bedfordians and a significant number of visitors from all over the place as well. The Cecil Higgins Gallery is, in my opinion, the jewel in the Crown of Bedford's visitor attractions. Situated on the banks of the Great Ouse, behind the Swan Hotel is the house where Higgins spent his early childhood. The house is furnished to resemble a Victorian home and was built in 1846 by

Cecil's grandfather. The old chap also built the brewery next door (now a museum). Cecil was born in 1856, he spent some time growing up (as we all do!) in Bedford, but (and this is important, so pay attention!) Cecil travelled and studied in Europe. On his return young Cecil ran the family brewing business but continued to collect ceramics and glass that he bequeathed to the town on the condition Bedford used it to start a museum. The Gallery was opened in 1949, eight years after Cecil Higgins death. You can wander through the house, view the fine collection of paintings, take in the wonderful furniture and fittings and just imagine what it must have been like to live in Victorian splendour. I am a simple soul and so I found the two papier-mache sofas quite incredible. The ceramics and glass are on display on the upper floors of the newer part of the gallery. Regular exhibitions of art are arranged and constantly changed. Considering that Bedford is a smallish town on the outskirts of London, the Cecil Higgins Gallery does a great job. They only have enough space to display just a small proportion of the pictures they own, and they are flexible enough to arrange for you to view what you want to see by previous appointment. Oh that other galleries were so forthcoming and helpful!

Cecil Higgins' house and museum showing the interior and part of his fine glass collection

Bedford Town Bridge over the River Great Ouse

The Cecil Higgins story done and dusted, 'Spainy' meandered along some three paces behind me (this is not through any sense of inferiority, just that he tends to fiddle with things and I am much more 'up and at 'em and let's get on with it'). " The Bishop of Bedford is a nice chap you know," I said, as something of a throwaway line, and not slackening pace. "Really", muttered my companion, "I think there's something wrong with one of my shutters." Focusing my eyes on the rowers puffing, blowing and generally exerting themselves in their narrow little craft on the River Ouse, I said (to myself), "There's a good chance both of his shutters will have problems before this journey is complete!"

Before we leave Bedford (because 'Spainy' is still devouring the contents of the kitchens at Bedford station), allow me to detail a small part of the town's history. The town is dominated by the river and began its history in Saxon times. By the year 886 (yes, it's that old) it was on the boundary that lay between that of the Danes and the kingdom of Alfred the Great. It was extended south of the river in 915 (for the benefit of our American cousins that is a year,

The Butterfly Bridge, Bedford

The Rainbow Bridge, Bedford

not a time!). After William the Conqueror came up from Hastings, a castle was built. There was a siege in 1224 and following the siege, eighty men were hung from the battlements, gruesome I know, but true. In the seventeenth century Bedford's river trade was developed, and only briefly interrupted by the Civil War (Yes, I hear our American cousins shouting "We had one of those!"). Bedford was best described as neutral, as far as the Civil War was concerned (always a good bet). With the restoration, religion became something of a 'hot potato' (as previously described). Bunyan was jailed and became probably Bedford's best known son. Terry Waite, the Beirut hostage carried with him a postcard of the Bunyan Window (to be found in the Independent church), and visited the town on his return to England.

Bedford is a bit of 'mix and match' really, the bus station is drab, parking in the town is difficult, shopping is quite good but not exceptional, pubs are a plenty, the ethnic mix is simply wonderful! Italian names above the restaurants are plentiful (Italian workers came after the Second World War to work in the brick industry). Visit and enjoy!

With the photographer part of the business firmly ensconced in the cafeteria at Bedford station and tucking into his second breakfast of the day. I took the opportunity to decide our next move, avoiding eating places of course!

John Bunyan's birthplace at Elstow is just a stone's throw from Bedford and it is worth a visit. The church and the Moot Hall give the feel of a village as it once clearly was. Elstow is a bus ride from Bedford town centre. Slightly further a field is Cardington, where two great airship hangars dominate the skyline. The famous airships were constructed here and the local (cathedral like) church relates the terrible story of the R101 that crashed in France on its maiden flight. The cemetery has a wonderful memorial. Cardington has a pub, standing at one end of the village green, in sight of the church and the house where John Howard (remember him?) once lived. A car ride (because public transport is somewhat depleted these days) away is the village of Old Warden. A certain Lord Ongley is the man responsible for the sheer beauty of this typical (?) English village. The thatched cottages look like something from the times of Elizabeth the First, but they are not! Ongley had them designed that way. Do not be put off, dear traveller. Visit Old Warden, tarry a while at the village pub and then trot off to Shuttleworth. I refuse to tell you more! (you can read about it in our first book!). Suffice to say that, if you visit and arrange things correctly, you will see (a) The Swiss Garden in all its splendour (b) Observe birds of prey as they are supposed to be seen, working with their handlers and (c) A matchless vintage aircraft collection. After all that, you can take tea in the restaurant, view the gardens of Shuttleworth House (Gothic and evocative) and still have the surrounding countryside to marvel at. So there we are then, all this within striking distance of the county town of Bedford, and we haven't even started our journey yet! For goodness sake, let's board that train and make for Luton. Luton! I hear you cry, why on earth would anyone in their right mind want to visit Luton? I have my reasons, so indulge me. Speaking of which (indulgence that is) what of my portly friend? Well he was still tucking into what remaining food the cafeteria staff at Bedford station had left! I bundled him onto the train and would, if they had been available, strapped him into his seat. "Where next" he asked, "Luton" I replied. "Why on earth would anyone want to visit Luton?" he asked. "That question has already been posed, so be quiet and look out of the window." So with that, he settled back into his seat and I ask you to do the same.

Airship hangars at Cardington

THE ENGLISH SCHOOL OF FALCONRY

I met Phil Gooden when I paid a visit to Shuttleworth to make some recordings. I know the Swiss Garden and Shuttleworth House very well, and have always felt that the wonderful gardens and lake make a perfect backdrop for someone who could come up with a way to utilise them. Phil has done just that! The son of a farmer, Phil was born in Huntingdon where he developed a love of the countryside. At the age of just five he was introduced to a friend of the family who was a Grand Falconer. Young Gooden took to working with birds of prey like a duck to water (forgive the sad joke); he happily cleaned the aviaries and learned about the husbandry and welfare of the birds. Aged twelve Phil was given a 'Lanner' falcon to fly. He eagerly embarked on learning the necessary techniques and by the age of twenty was displaying his and the bird's skills at country fairs. With his hard earned savings, he purchased other birds and continued to nurse his dream of owning his own bird of prey centre. Determined and professional Phil Gooden has finally achieved his dream, 'The English School of Falconry - Bird of Prey and Conservation Centre' is up and running, using that beautiful backdrop of gardens and lake I mentioned earlier. Emma Gooden, Phil's daughter moved with her family to the Woburn estate when she was five years old; dad couldn't wait to introduce to her to his passion for birds of prey. Emma's first bird, a Kestrel named 'Squeak' became her companion when she was nine years old. Just like dear old dad, Emma loves Falconry and everything to do with the countryside. She is responsible for preparing the notes for the flying displays, the literature which is supplied to groups who wish to learn about birds of prey as well as the welfare of her Vulture friend 'Vinnie'. Visit

'George' a Great Grey Owl

the school, take in the displays, fall in love as I did, with the birds, picnic by the lake where Swans rescued from other parts of the country are cared for. Now meet 'George'!

'George' is a Great Grey Owl, his Latin name is very posh - Strix Bebulosa. I am proud to tell you that I look forward to building a relationship with 'George' because I have adopted him. Very soon now George has an assignation planned with a female of his species. If we are lucky and the two lovebirds successfully breed, I will be a very satisfied gentleman! As you can see from his photo, George has a huge face, beautiful yellow eyes and the largest and most symmetrical disc of any owl. When I visit to have a chat with him, he says very little but I just know he understands every word I say!

Some of the birds at The English School of Falconry, Shuttleworth

'Spainy' resisted the temptation to fall asleep as the train left the station at Bedford, well actually he was assisted by several kicks in the shins from yours truly. "You might be required to take a few photographs," I informed him. You can still see a chimney or two as the train gathers speed through the Bedfordshire countryside. The chimneys are part of the story of Stewartby, a village named after the Stewart family. Built in 1926, the first houses had flushing loos! Now there's a thought! They also had a decent size garden and bathrooms. Is there no end to this domestic bliss? Well, actually there is and there isn't. The village itself is interesting from the point of view that the Stewart family built it to make bricks, it is not (I'm sorry to say) particularly good looking. Prior to 1935 the place was called Wootton Pillinge and, up until around 1926 was little more than a hamlet. There were eight cottages known as Forders Villas, these housed the key workers from the Pillinge Brickworks (owned by the Forders family), members of the Stewart family being among the company directors. It was the Stewart family's concern for their workers that brought about the 'Model Village', with only the families of brick workers allowed to rent the houses. The village Memorial Hall was built in 1929, paid for by the company and maintained by them, it also had a resident caretaker. Development continued until the outbreak of the Second World War and by then it had a swimming pool, two schools, a sports club, post office and a general store as well as a doctor's surgery. After the war more building took place. The distinguished architect Sir Albert Richardson designed some bungalows to be used solely by retired employees of the brick company, rent free. Interesting to reflect that this area of Bedfordshire should have been home to men of vision who had the needs of the common man at heart. Bunyan, Howard, Stewart and indeed Richardson, all left their mark, it must have been something in the water! And speaking of water, it is said that Mr Bunyan once washed his feet in Stewartby pond!

Talking of bricks. After the Second World War there was a great surge in the building industry in Britain and the demand for bricks grew. Geographically this made Bedford, situated close to the Oxford Clay Belt and already with a well established brick making industry, one of the obvious centres to expand. With the huge demand for building materials coupled with the overwhelming demand for labour in all other industries, there was a dangerous shortfall in the numbers of men to work in the area. In 1945 The Ministry of Labour mounted a national recruitment campaign aimed at Liverpool and Tyneside, unfortunately it failed and a comment at the time went something like this: "There is a desperate shortage of English labourers willing, in a time of affluence, to do the tough dirty work of the brickfields." By 1946 the government turned its attention to Eastern Europe by attempting to recruit mainly political refugees, but ended up producing another problem! Sadly these men were physically incapable of carrying out such work, either through poor health or by the fact that, they had previously worked as teachers, office workers etc. It has to be said, that they also faced some hostility from the indigenous population. While Britain was enjoying all this economic growth, Italy was experiencing problems. The living conditions in rural areas were particularly, to say the least, very poor. January 2nd, 1951 saw a meeting between the brick companies and the Ministry of Labour, and it was agreed that five hundred Italians would be recruited to work in the brickfields. So began the flow of Italian migrants to Bedfordshire. Italian P.O.W's had already been observed as being enterprising and effective and this may have assisted the decision. Interviews were conducted in southern Italy, men were asked, through interpreters, to stand naked on scales, and show the blisters on their hands as evidence of their life's hard work. In the long term it must have been clear to those engaged in bringing these workers into the area, that something would have to be done about the families they had left behind in the villages in Italy. With their men folk gone many of the villages began dying on their feet. Men returned to their homeland, others tried to bring their families to England. Over the years the Italian community in Bedford has grown and flourished and, indeed contributed richly to the town's everyday life.

Brickworks at Stewartby

As the train made its way to Luton my cumbersome friend clicked away with his camera, I continued to muse on the glories of the Bedfordshire countryside. It bears stating that the county has not enjoyed much in the way of recognition as far as tourism is concerned. Things are changing and rightly so, the villages have a lot to offer to the seasoned traveller who feels they have seen it all. The River Great Ouse wends its way across the county, and in Bedford, 'The Embankment' is a great place to amble and view the swans and ducks as well as the efforts of the rowers in their spindly boats. I have never understood rowing, it's a weird way to amuse yourself. All that sliding backwards and forwards on a little seat, wrenching your stomach muscles and then ending up out of breath and gasping. Far better to feed the remains of your sandwiches to the ducks and ponder on what life would have been like way back when the river was young. The river bridge at Great Barford, just a few miles from Bedford was constructed in the fifteenth century, it has seventeen arches. There's a pub nearby as well, perhaps that is why the Vikings liked the spot! It is, after all, a place they visited regularly. Just stand on the river's edge at Roxton or Tempsford for example, and through the mist and willow trees that overhang the water you can almost hear the slap of the oars as those violent campaigners paid another 'raping and pillaging' visit to our shores. Long after the Vikings had done their dastardly deeds and had been sent packing, the area became best known for its market gardens. In fact the first Brussels sprout to be grown in England appeared in a Bedfordshire field, now if that's not history in the making. I don't know what is! So before we continue our journey to Luton (Yes, I know you can't wait, but you must be patient!), let us tarry awhile to consider that you might like to spend more than a day in and around Bedford. Here then are some tips, arrange your visit before David Spain has rendered the area devoid of food! Hire a car, the villages are accessible by public transport but you would do better to take a car and stop for 'bed and breakfast' at one of the many pubs in the vicinity. Do take some time to partake of a glass or three at a village pub, you will find the locals very friendly, no inbreeding here!

The village pub and church in Great Barford

The bridge at Great Barford over the River Great Ouse

Places to Visit

Marston Vale Community Forest. In the heart of the county they have created a 250 acre country park. You can walk in it and feel the peace.

Marston Vale Community Forest:	**01234 767037**
The Cecil Higgins Gallery:	**01234 211222**
Bedford Museum:	**01234 353323**
Bedford Tourist Office:	**01234 215226**
The Swiss Garden:	**01767 627666**
The English School of Falconry:	**01767 627527**

CHAPTER 2 - A VIEW FROM THE WINDOW (LUTON BOUND, YES, WE ARE GETTING THERE!)

The train stops at Flitwick and it's but a 'lick and a spit' (a disgusting phrase, but I like it) to the Georgian town of Ampthill. I recommend you make the journey as Ampthill is full of interest, and will not disappoint the visitor. In the centre of the town at the cross-roads you will find the pump (1784) and close by is the Moot Hall, with a clock and cupola, rebuilt in 1852. Buildings full of history abound in this town and there is a wonderful garden to be found along the 'Kings Arms' yard, along with an avenue of Lime trees given to the town by Lord Holland in 1827. Sir John Cornwall built Ampthill Castle in the fifteenth century. King Henry Vll owned the property from 1508, and his son the notorious Henry Vlll quite liked it as well; he placed Katherine of Aragon in the castle while he waited to divorce her! Do find some time to visit Ampthill. If you are an American cousin, you will be interested to learn that there is a memorial in St. Andrews Church to a certain Richard Nicolls, the man who gave New York its name, he was born in Ampthill and lived most of his life in the town. Nicolls served the Stuart kings and named New York after the Duke of York, later King James 11. The memorial to Nicolls incorporates the Dutch cannon ball that claimed his life.

Wakey, Wakey 'Spainy', It's Flitwick! As for Flitwick (where the train stops for Ampthill as well), it is pleasant enough without being exceptional. Flitwick Moor is interesting, it is a nature reserve, partly rough pasture and grazed by cattle. Mostly it is an old peat working site, the peat being cut for use as fuel in days gone by. Because of the nature of the site the wildlife is of the minimal variety but worth preserving for all that. Sometime in the 19th century the water from the moor was bottled and sold (fraudulently), far better to drink the local ale! Oh yes, Billy Cotton, broadcaster and bandleader often arranged to play at 'The Corn Exchange', Bedford, so that he could visit his mother and father in Flitwick. He came from a working class background and his early musical experience came from being a bugle boy in the First World War. Later he was a pilot in the Royal Flying Corps. After the war 'our Bill' tried his hand at a number of different trades, he drove a bus, trained as a butcher, played football and was an amateur boxer. Finally Bill joined a dance band as a drummer. He formed his own band and by 1928 was a firm favourite with audiences. He topped the bill in the West End club 'Ciros' that was, at the time, a haunt of the Prince of Wales (later to become King Edward VIII). Cotton developed comedy in his act and included several rather 'naughty' songs in his repertoire. At about this time his parents retired to Flitwick. Billy Cotton's son, another Bill as you may recall, who became Head of Light Entertainment at the BBC, remembers visiting his grandparents at the oil lit house in Flitwick. As late as 1928, the Flitwick Council had voted against installing gas, electricity or water and sewerage on the basis of cost, what a farsighted council that must have been! By 1935 Billy Cotton, bandleader had become Billy Cotton, racing driver and he frequently drove at Silverstone which is about thirty miles from Flitwick. His band toured with ENSA during the Second World War. After the war appearances at the London Palladium re-established his career and he became a really big star through his Sunday lunchtime broadcasts on BBC Radio. I grew up with the dulcet tones of Billy Cotton, singer Alan Breeze and the rest of the crew, so I didn't think twice when 'Spainy' tried to doze off. "Wakey, Wakey!"

The Flitwick Manor Hotel

So What of Harlington?

It's the next stop on the line and you may remember (keep up for goodness sake!) that one John Bunyan was arrested and brought here in 1660, for preaching at nearby Lower Samshill. There are a couple of pubs in the village worth a visit and close by there was an Oak tree where Bunyan is supposed to have preached; a sapling has been planted beside the dead tree. The church of St. Mary is late thirteenth century, the windows are sixteenth century and the nave roof fifteenth century. Notice the corbel that depicts a man leading a dragon by a rope around its neck while another dragon attacks him.

Sharpenhoe 'Clappers'

Harlington Church

Harlington has several timber framed houses and it's a rather good place to begin a walk in the area, not the least because, if you make your walk circular, you start and end at a pub! Come to think of it, if you spend too much time at the bar, your walk is likely to be circular anyway! Close to Harlington there is the site of an Iron Age camp at Sharpenhoe Clappers, and there is a fine view across the Chiltern Hills as well. The village of Sharpenhoe nestles neatly at the foot of the Clappers. Thomas Norton, a forerunner of Shakespeare was buried at Streatley (close by) in 1584. I just knew you would want to know what 'Clappers' are, well, for once I'm not sure, but it has something do with rabbits and the French, don't even think about it!

THEN THERE IS LUTON!

Despite 'Spainy' moaning and groaning we made it to Luton and, in order to placate my friend I took him directly to the Hardware Café. The 'Hardware' is a ten minute walk from the town centre (and well known to me because it is where I eat before broadcasting). 'Spainy' was out of breath when we arrived, so I had to place our order. "I will have scrambled eggs on two slices of toast and a cup of tea and he will have everything else you have in the kitchen." Suitably refreshed we made our way to Luton Town Centre.

If you are the type of person who thinks that Luton is a dreary place where very little goes on and that there is nothing to see, then you are David Spain's sort of person and I am about to prove you wrong.

When Lorraine Chase made the TV advert and uttered those immortal words, "Nah, Luton airport." She didn't realise it but she was placing an image of the town in people's minds. Luton has been fighting to change that image ever since. A quick rundown of places to visit, reveals plenty to do and see. The town centre is a not very pleasant mixture of the modern and not so modern. As you amble through from the station to the Hardware Café take the opportunity to look above the shop fronts.

The 'famous' Hardware Cafe

14

J.P. with some of Luton's firefighters

Luton Museum

Luton 'Hoo'

Fred Stoughton and his dog at 'Somaries'

Somaries Tudor Castle

Luton Airport

And so, back to the station and on to Harpenden and also back to trying to keep 'Spainy' awake, and back to trying to arrange an itinerary which avoids eating places. By the time this book is finished he won't be able to make it through a turnstile in one trip!

Most of the people who live there will tell you that Harpenden is a village, and you can't blame them for that. You probably get that 'village' feel because the Common has been preserved along with the cricket pitch and other green areas. The coming of the railways led to Harpenden's rapid growth and there is a small Railway Museum well worth visiting. This is no run of the mill museum, it's in Geoff Woodward's back garden! No steam trains running on a mile or two of track, rather memorabilia collected over the years. From seats to signals, platform barrows, seats, signals and lamps, you can view it all, but only on special open days.

Take a look at these photos below.

Harpenden is a pleasant place with plenty of shops, restaurants and pubs, the church of St Nicholas is worth a visit as well. But I have directed you to Harpenden to view the last resting place of a man who is said to have been at the very centre of the plot to put an innocent man behind bars on Devils Island, the notorious French Penal Colony. On a morning in May, 1923 there was a burial at Harpenden parish churchyard, it was a simple affair, witnessed, it is said by just seven mourners, a priest and the grave digger. The coffin, with brass fittings bore the inscription 'Count Jean de Voilemont, died May 21st 1923, aged 74 years'. It turns out that the occupant of the coffin was no Count at all! The man they buried on that spring morning was none other than Major Esterhazy, said to be the person whose evidence sent Major Alfred Dreyfus to Devils Island. At the time Harpenden was said to be shocked to its roots. The man the locals had known as the 'Count' was in fact the very same person who had been a spy for the Germans in the 1800's and indeed responsible, along with others for inventing the evidence on which Alfred Dreyfus, an officer in the French Artillery was convicted of treason

The grave of 'Count' de Voilemont

and sent to Devils Island. In order to shield both himself and others from suspicion of treason Esterhazy and friends successfully diverted the authorities attention to Dreyfus. A co-conspirator of Esterhazy a man known simply as 'Henry' was arrested and sent to prison but was later found dead in his cell. Before Esterhazy was called to give evidence he had fled the country. In 1906 Dreyfus was found innocent of all charges. As for Esterhazy, well he reappeared in Harpenden as 'Count' de Voilemont. The 'Count' was often seen riding his horse on Harpenden Common, and his lady wife the 'Countess' was regularly seen shopping in the village. The Ezterhazy's lived at 'The Elms' in Station Road, Harpenden, but later they moved to 'Homeleigh' in Milton Road. The 'village grapevine' suggested that the 'Count' was a German spy; a certain Mr Gordon (now long departed) is said to have reported hearing Morse Code being tapped out from the 'Counts' home. A walking stick said to be owned by Esterhazy was discovered after his death. The ornate handle unscrewed to reveal a hollow section designed (it is presumed) to conceal secret papers. Just to cloud the issue further, the secret service is said to have been aware of the 'Counts' whereabouts and that he volunteered to visit Germany as a spy during the First World War. We may never know the true story but we do know that the man in question is buried in Harpenden.

Locally you can't mention Harpenden without mentioning the 'Nicky Line' (you can try but enthusiasts wouldn't let you get away with it). There is little doubt that, like many another town, Harpenden expanded rapidly with the coming of the railway. There is still evidence of the days of steam and the Lea Valley Walk follows the route of the old Great Northern branch line, but it is the 'Nicky Line' that was a branch line to Hemel Hempstead, belonging to the Midland Railway Company, which is most fondly remembered. It was opened on 16th July 1877 and ran a passenger service to and from Luton, as well as carrying goods traffic (the railway had been planned to service the straw plait industry at Luton but by the time the branch line had been built, this industry had declined). It is said that Winston Churchill held meetings in a train on the line during the war years. Regular bus services were

Harpenden Church

the cause of passenger services being withdrawn in 1947 but goods and freight services continued until closure in 1963. From 1968, a private company was allowed to operate its own freight train until 1979, when the controlling signal box at Harpenden was closed. Although the tracks have gone, it is still possible to walk or cycle along most of the former branch line between the two towns.

'Rothamsted', Harpenden

Chapter 3 - On the Subject of Falling Asleep!

I have already informed you that 'Spainy' tends to nod off on a train, I have to be honest and inform you that I joined him! Following our visit to Harpenden we boarded the train with the intention of travelling to Mill Hill. I awoke as the train passed Tulse Hill! 'Spainy' was gazing out of the window, "Where are we?" I asked. "On our way to London" came his reply, "Why didn't you wake me up?" "You looked so peaceful and anyway I've never been to Gatwick." I hesitated for a moment before asking my friend what Gatwick had to do with it? "This train goes through to Gatwick airport and I thought we might take a look." Knowing how quickly 'Spainy' can go into a sulk if he fails to get his own way, I decided to negotiate. "I wouldn't mind taking a look at Crawley." So we did and it's a good thing we did, not because Crawley or Gatwick are anything special but because, on the way back we discovered somewhere worth visiting in Tulse Hill!

But First, Crawley and Gatwick

Think Crawley, think Gatwick, think Gatwick, think airport and not much else! On the other hand, think Crawley, think New Town and nothing else! In fact and just in case you have arrived at London Gatwick, and are thinking of moving on rather quickly, you would do well to take a look at the area surrounding the airport. Crawley, or to give the place its original name, 'craw leah', received its charter from King John in 1202 (that's a date, not a time!). OK so maybe 'craw leah' does mean a crow infested field, you can't have everything can you? Nevertheless (and if you enjoy making tenuous links) it's nice to know that the place has always been associated with wings and flying! In times gone by Crawley was quite important as a coaching stop, being roughly half way between London and the south coast. There is still some evidence of medieval buildings, but not much, it has to be said. However, and with Crawley as your starting point, you could visit NYMANS GARDENS at Handcross near Haywards Heath. The gardens are owned by the National Trust and are described as, "One of the great gardens of the Sussex Weald" (just in case, like me, you wondered what a weald is, it's a term used in Sussex, Kent and Surrey meaning a wooded area). You can visit Lady Rosse's library as well as the distinctive garden with its woodland walks. Telephone: 01444 400321 or 01444 400777 for more details.

WAKEHURST PLACE: In 1205 William de Wakehurst purchased some land from Philip de Craule (another spelling of Crawley). There is evidence of habitation much earlier than de Craule but you can find that out for yourself when you visit, I'M NOT DOING EVERYTHING FOR YOU! In 1454 two brothers named Culpeper are said to have forcibly abducted two sisters, Margaret and Elizabeth from their guardian. Since the girls were the last of the Wakehurst line, that's a family, not a railway. One can only imagine what a hornets nest the Culpepers stirred up.

You may well be surprised to learn that the marriages were both rather happy and the two families lived at Wakehurst from 1464. Another member of the Culpeper family was the herbalist, Nicholas. Thomas Culpeper died in 1571 leaving orders that the house needed to be rebuilt, I guess that you can do that when you die, leave orders for other people. His son, Edward carried out his father's wishes. In 1694 the estate was sold to, a friend of Samuel Pepys the diarist, Dennis Lydell who was a commissioner of the Navy. Over the ensuing years Wakehurst has seen many owners and various bits have been added to the house. Quite apart from the house itself there is much to see and do at Wakehurst. The Millennium Seed Bank Project is one of the biggest conservation projects ever undertaken. At Wakehurst the Royal

Botanic Gardens, Kew have constructed new seed vaults for conservation, research and education. You can walk the Dinosaurs Dinner Trail, or amble the Birch Trail and the National Collection of Birches is held at Wakehurst Place. If all this is not enough to satisfy your horticultural and historical appetite, then seek a 'Brief Encounter'. This is for people who have only a short amount of time and gives you a taste of some of the best sites at Wakehurst.

HOW TO GET THERE

The nearest railway station is HAYWARDS HEATH, trains are frequent and Wakehurst is just six miles from the station and served by several bus routes. For more information on Wakehurst you can telephone: 01444 894066

LET'S RETURN TO CRAWLEY FOR A CREEPY TALE

To those who knew him, John Haigh was a reasonable sort of chap, well spoken and with an interest in music. Haigh moved to Crawley in 1943, he rented a workshop in Leopold Road in the West Green district of the town. Even after he returned to live in London, Haigh maintained links with Crawley, as it turned out, in more ways than one! Haigh was arrested in February 1949 and charged with the murder of a woman. As the story unfolded, it was alleged that the woman was shot in the Leopold Road workshop and that Haigh had dissolved her body in a bath of acid. Acid, a gun and some rubber gloves were found at the address in Crawley and it is said that Haigh retired to the 'Ancient Priors' in the town to take tea while the unfortunate lady's remains were dissolving. Haigh was tried in Lewes and eventually hanged on August 10th 1949. So, with the gruesome tale of Mr Haigh ringing in our ears Mr Spain and I returned to the railway station.

Since I have mentioned Haywards Heath, 'Spainy' has decided to include a picture from his 'archives'. This shows a photo of the 'Bleriot' monoplane at Haywards Heath in 1912. As you will see, the plane is due to take off to cross the English Channel to France. I allowed 'Spainy' to include this photo because he was probably there at the time!

'Bleriot' monoplane at Haywards Heath, 1912

Now then, on the Subject of Cemeteries!

I quite like cemeteries, not only do they tend to be peaceful places, but they stimulate the mind. One can wander freely reading the inscriptions on the headstones and ponder on what type of person is buried below (usually a dead person, I hear you cry), but you know what I mean - if you believe the old adage, 'You can tell a man by the clothes he wears' then what, I ask myself do you make of the man, or woman from the headstone or inscription they have displayed to the world? Naturally, the headstone may well say more about those that the deceased has left behind but, at least it gives some sort of an insight.

Just a ten minute walk from Tulse Hill railway station and on the way back from Gatwick where, you may recall we had never intended to be in the first place! You will find West Norwood Cemetery and 'Spainy' being 'Spainy' and me, being me, we decided to take a look around . Our visit to West Norwood proved to be an illuminating experience. We had just walked through the main gates and were gazing at the final resting place of one, Sir Hiram Maxim (1840 - 1916) when we heard a cockney voice, "There are plenty of interesting people in here mate," we turned to see a well dressed, elderly man walking towards us. Now I am quite a friendly soul most of the time, but I admit that I was rather looking forward to an hour or two wandering the cemetery with David taking photographs and didn't fancy any interruptions, how glad I am that I took the time to smile at our interrupter. "I visit the graves of a few old friends from the war every Sunday morning before the pub opens," I was informed. Not only did my seventy six year old friend visit his old mates, but he also had a few words for his ex - wife, who it turned out was buried in an unmarked grave. Let me explain, this veteran of 'D' Day and many other World War Two escapades had married the love of his life many years ago, they didn't get on very well (she being much younger than he) and they parted. "She took well over thirty thousand pounds from our divorce and married a man more than half her own age," our companion told us as we walked towards a bare patch of grass among the wobbly headstones. "When she died her new husband took the money and didn't even bother to have her grave marked." I resisted the temptation to ask just why our friend saw fit to visit the lady every Sunday, or indeed, why he hadn't bothered to mark her final resting place. I resisted because, after a very brief moment spent gazing at a bare patch of grass, he launched into a 'Rough Guide' of the cemetery.

Entrance gate to West Norwood Cemetery

Off We Go Then! A List of Just Some of the Notables Buried in West Norwood.

Sir Hiram Maxim: one of our esteemed American cousins, born in Sangeville, Maine, U.S.A. in 1840, died London, England 1916. The eldest son of a farmer, Maxim was apprenticed to a carriage maker. He was nothing short of a genius, obtaining his first patent in 1866 (for a curling iron). He went on to invent a device for generating illuminating gas and a locomotive headlight as well as several rather technical devices. Maxim had an interest in automatic weapons and moved to London where, in 1884 he produced the first fully automatic gun. You might, at this stage begin to wonder whether he should have bothered, but if he hadn't someone else would have and anyway such is the way of the world. Within a few short years, every army was equipped with Maxim guns or adaptations. In the 1890's Hiram experimented with aeroplanes but, what with one thing and another he discontinued this line of thinking. A mousetrap and an automatic sprinkling system took up some of his time and in 1884 he formed what was to become the Vickers Company Ltd. In 1900 he became a naturalised British subject and he was knighted by Queen Victoria in 1901. What an absolutely fascinating dinner guest he must have been!

The grave of Sir Hiram Maxim, 1840 - 1916

Cubes and Cubism!

Sir Henry Tate 1819 - 1899 was born in Chorley, Lancashire and entered the sugar trade in Liverpool. He invented a way of cutting sugar into cubes and made his fortune! Tate moved to London in 1880 and was a great social benefactor. He is particularly remembered for his gift of the National Gallery of British Art to the nation. One hesitates to make the link between Cubism and sugar. One hesitates but cannot resist. One cannot also resist the temptation to ask exactly why all the great inventors and businessmen of the Victorian era simply could not resist offering money for good causes? Could it be that they had somehow, more of a sense of wanting to be remembered or is that just too cynical?

The mausolea of Sir Henry Tate (above) and Sir Henry Doulton (below)

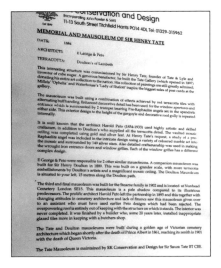

Grave of the original Mrs Beeton

'Spainy' in the cemetery? Why is he out during daylight?

You can spend many a contemplative hour wandering the cemetery. Take a special look at the Greek Cemetery that contains a large collection of mausolea. The main mausoleum being that of Augustus Ralli who died in 1872. The mortuary chapel that dominates the Greek Cemetery is described in the cemetery guide as a complete freak, it is quite beautiful.

Guided tours are available on Sunday afternoons during the Summer

Greek Cemetery

CHAPTER 4 - MEMORIES AND REFLECTIONS

Listeners to the 'Out and About' radio programme never cease to amaze me with stories of their youth and while it is good to hear their stories on the airwaves, it is all the better when I get to meet them. So it was that David Spain and I visited James Perry at his Welwyn Garden City home. 'Spainy' took a couple of photographs as James and I sat down to record some of his memories of the Second World War. For the purposes of this book and for reasons not possible to discuss here, I have taken James' written memories and tried to tell them as he told them to me. First, a brief history of the Chindits will assist us to get the story into focus: **Orde Charles Wingate was born in India , he was educated at Charterhouse and Royal Military Academy. He was commissioned and served in the Sudan. At one time he served as an intelligence officer in Palestine and organised night patrols to repel Arab raids on Jewish communities. From January to May 1941 Wingate led an Ethiopian-Sudanese force which took Addis Ababa from the Italians. He formed the "Chindits" and helped to train a similar American force known as "Merrill's Marauders". During May 1943 the "Chindits" entered Japanese held Burma, crossing the Chindwin River, they received supplies by air and appeared to be quite effective in their guerrilla campaign. Since the war, and with hindsight, there has been much discussion as to the effectiveness of Wingate's campaign and indeed the manner in which his troops were treated.**

James Perry is over eighty years of age and, when David Spain and I visited, he greeted us dressed in his green blazer covered in badges and campaign emblems.

JAMES PERRY'S MEMORIES

"As a member of the Bedfordshire and Hertfordshire Regiment and having volunteered for the far east I found myself in Bristol. We boarded a large transport ship with its port of registration

erased. As I clambered up the gangplank someone shouted, "How long were you in for mate?" "Same as you mate" I replied, "For the duration." I wasn't aware of the terms of his question. It turned out that we were taking aboard criminals from our prisons. With the hatches battened down and the stench rising from them, these men were shackled twenty to a chain. I saw a young man fall from the ship's rail into the sea. I told my friend (a pickpocket) that no man could have climbed the rail he answered, "Stop that talk or you will be next." The prisoners who were to become troops had rules of their own. We had fifteen nurses on board and we heard a rumour that some of the men had plans to rape them. The history of the regiment seems to have omitted some of the scenes I witnessed, years later I still awoke to the screams of women being raped."

James went on to tell us about a mutiny that took place in India, he says that the men felt that the food was so bad they couldn't eat it. They stampeded the pack horses by firing blanks into the air. I found my interview with James very difficult, clearly he experienced some terrible events during the Second World War. I wanted so much to report his memories, wanted to do them justice. Unfortunately, James written memories are a little confused as are his spoken memories. In no way should this detract from the fact that I met a very brave man on the morning I visited his home. Proud to this very day of his contribution, not in the least bitter of the punishments which he and his mates incurred from his own officers behind enemy lines. I am left to wonder if we ever really know the real truth of what some of our troops endured during the Second World War. I do know that I believed every single word James Perry told me, do know that it was a desperate and stinking war they fought, I respect James Perry, I am grateful to him and his generation, can't tell you about some of the stories he related to me. They were, quite simply too disjointed, some of them, too terrible, I can't substantiate all of them, although, I have spoken to contacts who will not discount them. James Perry is mentioned in the book about the Chindits entitled 'March Or Die' by Philip D. Chinnery. I thank James for allowing me into his home, I thank him for what he and his mates did for me and my generation. I make no apology for including what appears to be a somewhat incomplete explanation of James Perry's memories, I simply felt that we owe him something.

A Nine Year Old Evacuee

Bill Collins lives in Milton Keynes and he told me the story of his trip to Canada as a nine year old lad.

"In August 1939 I went with my mum, brother and little sister to a park for a picnic. I remember that the park was opposite Fairey Aviation where my dad was working at the time. Dad was going to meet us at mid-day, but one of his mates came instead to tell us that dad had been called up by the Territorial Army. We had some pretty bad times in the mid thirties, dad had not been in work and we were just getting on our feet when the war came. In later years I asked dad why he sent us to Canada, he said that he was convinced that it was the correct thing to do when he was posted to Anglesey to help defend it against invasion, they had just one three inch gun for the whole island!

Meanwhile, we were issued with gas masks, had an Anderson shelter built in the back garden and received our ration books. We had some air raids but no bombs. Mum told me that I wouldn't go to sleep and that, when it was time for school I was dog tired. We kids had our names put forward when the Children's Overseas Reception Board was formed in 1940. We went to stay near the Ack, Ack battery where my dad was close to Coventry. I think that it was around the time of Dunkirk that my dad took us to the theatre, we saw Vera Lynn, there was a sense of being British and alone, but all together and it even rubbed off on us kids.

In July 1940 my brother and I had our medical to go to Canada, we got our papers to go late in July and the Red Cross kitted us out because our own clothes were rags. I got a pair of cricket boots! I loved them because I could make sparks with the studs in the soles. Mum took out a loan with a local credit draper to get us some more decent clothes, he trusted my mum and became a long standing family friend.

My dad got leave to see us off and on the seventh of August 1940 we left Stockport for Glasgow, mum couldn't face seeing us off and, since dad had to return to his unit immediately, he wasn't able to console her. We seemed to travel all over the country picking kids up, we got to see Edinburgh castle! Camp beds were laid out in a school in Glasgow and we were given a round of bread and a bowl of broth. For three or four days we were fed like kings.

On August the eleventh we were taken to the docks to board the 'Duchess of York', we were stationed in the belly of the ship. In the dining room the tables were laid with table cloths, lots of silver and big white menus, the steward became irritated because we couldn't decide what to choose from the menu. We decided to order everything! On the twelfth of August we sailed down the Clyde, we passed a warship coming in with a great hole in its side, we all rushed to the side to cheer the Royal Navy. I never did find out the name of the ship. We spent our time doing boat drills and certain areas were reserved for paying passengers but we seemed to have the run of the ship. My cricket boots clattered in unison with the Geordie and Scottish lads!

The captain got a bit annoyed with us when our gang (about fifty strong), threw a large rocking house over the side and shouted, "Look a sea horse." We did get into a great deal of trouble one way or another and finally the captain threatened to lock us in the brig! After eleven days we arrived in Halifax, Nova Scotia, another lad and I were filmed pretending to write postcards home. The Canadian people were so generous to us, showering us with sweets and cakes. It took us all of one night and into the next day to pass Lake Superior. We thought Canada was all cowboys and Indians, we had only seen pictures at the cinema! We were very lucky to have arrived safely.

Hitler had resolved to intensify the air war and naval blockade of Great Britain on the first of August 1940. The new blockade area was extended to the North Atlantic to twenty degrees West. U boats were free to attack without warning. The Volendam carrying six hundred and six passengers of whom three hundred and twenty one were sponsored sea evacuees, left Liverpool for Halifax on the twenty ninth of August. On the thirtieth the Volendam was torpedoed, only the Purser was lost, eighteen lifeboats were launched and all but one evacuee, aged nine years, slept through it all! Waking up to find the ship afloat but empty he went back to bed! The successful rescue may have lulled the authorities into a false sense of security. Three hundred and twenty one children had escaped and three hundred and nineteen were sent home to allow their parents time to reconsider. Michael Brooker of Bromley and Patricia Allen of Liverpool were added to the next sailing, the ship was the City of Benares. On September thirteenth, 1940 The City of Benares sailed at 1p.m. On the seventeenth the escort, one destroyer and two sloops withdrew - judging Convoy OB213 to be in safe waters. As night fell a force five gale was blowing. Around 10p.m. six hundred miles from the British coast, U Boat 48 released a five hundred pound torpedo that hit the ship and exploded in number five hold. Eighty three of the ninety two children on board were lost. We were indeed very lucky!"

Meet Ollie from the Watford Observer

David Spain works quite closely with the local press and it turned out that we share a mutual acquaintance. And so it was that I turned up in Cassiobury Park, Watford to record an interview with a certain Mr Oliver Phillips who had been recommended as the man who knows more about Watford than anyone else. Ollie, as he is known to his colleagues on The 'Watford Observer' newspaper has become something of a fixture in Watford. His reporting on Watford FC has spanned four decades. He made his first team debut in 1962. "I was very nervous the first time, but Cliff Holton scored a hat-trick against Watford, his old club, so the story more or less wrote itself. Ollie has produced a number of highly collectible supplements on the history of Watford, and the nostalgia page in the newspaper provides answers to readers questions. Ollie also takes a look at life and people in his other column 'Just A Word'. He says, "I've never had a Monday morning feeling. The remuneration in weekly newspapers is not great, but enjoying your job and looking forward to it for more than forty years is worth a lot in itself." In his time he has verbally wrestled with a couple of chairmen of Watford FC, clashed with managers such as Dave Bassett and not only reflected the history of the club but influenced it as well, by introducing Elton John to Vicarage Road!

"It was a particularly difficult time politically, so I encouraged Elton, who harboured ambitions for the club to take a relatively low profile as a pop star indulging his whim and trying to help the club by way of a concert. That way he got in at the ground floor without alerting suspicions of the then chairman, who felt threatened by anyone appearing to have a greater income, in case they were seeking to take over the club." Three years later Elton John took over Watford and returned the compliment when he attended the book launch of Ollie's 'History of Watford Football Club', which just happened to outsell 'The Joy of Sex'!

When asked what his most satisfying moment has been during his forty one years in local journalism, Ollie cites his series on Sandringham Road, where a German V1 flying bomb exploded with disasterous results. "I had eleven names of the victims and nowhere could I find an official record of who had died, despite it being one of the biggest single flying bomb disasters of the war. It became part research, part detective story and hours of checking and cross-checking. It took over my life for three months or more and although we ran a series for twelve weeks, it was not until the seventh week, that I had a breakthrough and finally had all the names I needed as well as some anecdotes to go with them." Watford Council were suitably impressed and made alterations to their disaster memorial on the strength of Ollie's reports.

Wearing his trademark 'Fedora', Ollie travels the length and breadth of the country covering Watford Football Club and their games. On one occasion he was flown to Florida by Elton John for an interview, and collected at the airport by a stretch limo with seats so soft, "I wondered where my bum had gone." Ollie Phillips is a real character without doubt. Not only has he spent a great deal of time with Elton John, but there have been several dinners and chats with Watford manager, Graham Taylor (who retired at the end of last season), some of them when they drank rather too much wine! Ollie's current project is his second book, 'The Golden Boys' featuring heroes of Watford Football Club, which is to be published in the Autumn of 2001.

Ollie interviewing the Watford FC Chairman Elton John

"Cassiobury Park Gates were demolished" - both J.P. and Ollie agree it was a bad mistake!

THE OLD GAOL, BUCKINGHAM

The Old Gaol Museum is well worth a visit if you go to Buckingham town centre. It was one of the first purpose-built county gaols in England and is now a museum showing aspects of Buckingham's proud history.

Open: Monday - Saturday 10:00am - 4:00pm all year round.

(Please telephone for Sunday opening hours.)

For information telephone: 01280 823020

The Old Gaol, Buckingham

THE BUCKS AIRCRAFT RECOVERY GROUP

I mentioned BARG in our last book but we didn't give it enough coverage in my view and (oddly, because it is a milestone in our relationship) 'Spainy' agreed. The Bucks Aircraft Recovery Group comprises of some keen men and women who work tirelessly in pursuit of their interest. It is not simply a group formed to recover pieces of wartime aircraft. BARG members are dedicated to keeping alive the memory of those who fought and in some cases, gave their lives for their country. At the time of writing BARG have had to store a great deal of their exhibits owing to the current re-structuring at Bletchley Park, Milton Keynes, which has been their home for some years. If and when you get the chance to visit, you will be stunned to see the array of aircraft engines, wing pieces, flying uniforms, guns, and ammunition, the list is endless. You will also more than likely find a member of BARG who can relate first hand their war experiences. BARG members, young and not so young are to be congratulated for helping to maintain the important 'human' part of the history of war for those of us who were fortunate enough not to experience it at first hand.

AND SPEAKING OF FIRST HAND STORIES:

Jack Bromfield is a member of BARG who can relate story after story about his wartime experiences. A Bletchley man born and bred, Jack has that somewhat diffident air about him when he tells you that he bailed out of his aircraft, stayed on the run for eight days and then became a reluctant resident at a German POW camp! If you press him he will go into more detail, we pressed him.

Jack Bromfield in an interview with J.P.

"As a train reporter, working at Bletchley station I was in a reserved occupation and found out that the only way I could join up was by volunteering for aircrew. Prior to that I was in the Air Training Corps. I wanted to be a pilot, but that wasn't to be. At Cardington, Bedfordshire in December 1942 we were asked to demonstrate our Morse Code skills, most of the blokes could handle about six words a minute but because of my railway training I tapped merrily away at somewhere around thirteen. That did it! They thanked me and sent me off to train as a wireless operator."

And so began the train of events that would culminate in a horrendous experience on January 5th 1944. Jack takes up the story:

"Some six hundred or so aircraft set out for Hanover on a raid, there were Halifaxs, Lancasters and Mosquitos; my Halifax "S" for "Sugar" was out of commission, so that night we given "Q" - Queenie." George Dacey, who was a replacement member of the crew had remained somewhat quiet at the briefing, particularly when a mate of Jack Bromfield's casually asked, "If you don't come back can I have your egg." Such was the tension of the job, these boys tended to have a rather blasé attitude! Anyway, "Q" - Queenie took off with Bromfield and the rest of the crew concentrating on the job in hand.

"A few miles from the target, just when we were getting set to deliver our bombs and then turn from home the rear gunner reported a Ju-88 fighter approaching. I didn't hear the warning but I pretty soon realised that we were being attacked, because this was when was when my knackers felt as they had been dragged up around my neck! Our plane had gone into a violent corkscrew, at the bottom of the roll, the aircraft made a steep climb and this time my balls dipped to my ankles!"

Jack continued to tell his story in his matter of fact manner. In all the plane corkscrewed three times and then levelled out, they had failed to shake off the fighter and Bromfield heard a mighty bang as an armour piercing shell burst through the fuselage, the shell continued its journey through the plane, passing just a foot away from Jack's arm!

"I clambered from my position to take a look around, above the bomb bay a fire was going strong. We were in a gentle dive, the aircraft was not responding and it was clear that "Q" - Queenie was done for. The skipper gave the order to bale out! I took a couple of parachutes from a locker, handed one to my mate and tried to open the escape hatch only to find that it had been damaged in the attack and I had to lay on top to try to get it open. Someone behind me thought I was stuck so they gave me a boot in the back and out I went, hatch and all!"

Some of the crew had problems, the rear gunner decided to avoid the fire and turned his turret to the side and jumped. Robertson, the pilot was a big chap, as he clambered out of his seat the ring on his parachute caught on something, yards of silk billowed out into the cockpit. Snatching as much of the parachute into a bundle Robertson, well aware that he was likely to be dragged up into the propellers, jumped! His chute opened safely and he drifted to earth. Meanwhile our Jack had opened his chute at around fifteen thousand feet and he was surprised to see a large object chasing him down to earth, it turned out to be the aircraft survival dinghy.

"I landed on my arse and quickly hid my parachute and cleared off into the darkness as quickly as I could. Nobody realised until much later that young Dacey had not made it."

Sucking his Horlicks tablets, Jack walked until day dawned, then took refuge in the woods to wait for nightfall again.

"I decided to cross the river and pick up the railway line, it was easy, the bridge was guarded but the gantry wasn't. I took the road west to Sulingen. As time passed, I decided to chance travelling by day, I was sick and tired of falling into potholes. At one time I saw seven men with their hands on their heads

and armed civilians but they moved off in the opposite direction. About half way to the Dutch border I arrived at a small railway station, I was ravenous and took a chance. I was just about to make a feast of a pile of Swedes when I heard a cry of "Hands Up!" It was the stationmaster, he took me to the signal box, cum office cum waiting room and made a phone call. Two hours later having remained free for eight days without help and deep behind enemy lines I was finally in the hands of the Luftwaffe."

PS: Jack Bromfield's story can be found among many others in a book by Mel Rolfe entitled, 'Hell on Earth'. When 'Hell on Earth' was published Jack Bromfield found out exactly who had kicked him out of the aircraft! He has since spoken to the offender Jock Laurie for the first time since that fateful night in 1944.

BARG members searching for wreckage

About two years ago some of the members of BARG decided to pay a visit to Ireland, their purpose was to take a look at a mountainous site in County Kerry. Mount Brandon is on the west coast of Ireland and is just about the last stop before America! The group knew that four aeroplanes had crashed on the mountain in the Second World War. Dave the Thatcher takes up the story:

"We took the boat from Fishguard to Rosslere, then drove to Portlaoise, we stayed with one of our group's mum and dad and after a meal we were taken to one of the many bars to be taught how to drink Guinness properly! The next day we made the long drive through Limerick to Tralee, on to Cloghone in

County Kerry. We took rooms and a meal at O'Connor's Bar and Guest House and asked how we could find the German Focke Wulf 200 Condor that we knew had crashed nearby. It happened that the bar runs the local mountain rescue team and they have an engine from the aircraft in their car park! We went off to the mountain and after about an hour we found the undercarriage legs and one of the engines, we searched through the scree and found other smaller parts of the aircraft. That night, after dinner we looked at old newspaper cuttings that had been collected by the pub owners and we talked to locals. One of the regulars had been photographed at the wreck site at the time. He was also in a photo at the site, on the mountain where a Sunderland had crashed. The next day we drove to the other side of the mountain where we made the long walk to where two Sunderlands and a Vickers Wellington were supposed to be. This was Ireland! And the rain poured down! After two hours hard walking we found pieces of wreckage spread over an area of about half a mile. Among the items we found were some pieces of china, bottles, a shoe brush and a jacket button with the Imperial Airlines design on it. This plane was the Short Sunderland "G-AGES" which crashed on 29th July 1943, it was operated by British Overseas Airways and was bringing the very first letters from prisoners of war in the Far East. After the crash local people went up to the site and gathered the letters, they sent them on to England. It turned out that the man in the bar the previous night had been one of that party. It was still raining! We searched for another four hours but found nothing else. On our return to the bar we had a meal, chatted to the locals and had the odd drink. The next morning I blamed my thick head on the peat fire! We returned to England and the following Monday evening I was telling my mates in our local about our trip. One of them told me that he had some letters at home sent by his dad from Thailand where he had been a POW. Would you believe it! One of those very letters had been on that Sunderland flight! It had been picked up by one Tom Kennedy Brandon on the crash site and sent on. I have a copy of that very letter."

Dave, Martin and their colleagues at BARG are to be commended for keeping alive the memories of those wartime years, the men and women who fought and in some cases, gave their lives.

A group of BARG members in Ireland

Canned Food and Pyramids

Ken Haughton is a regular listener and regular contributor to the 'Out and About' programme. We got to talking about food in cans one day, I don't know why Ken telephoned the show but after listening to him I asked him to write down his memories:

"Nearly sixty years ago I was serving in the British Army in the Middle East, some fifteen miles from Cairo. Our camp was within site of the River Nile and the great pyramids at Giza, the Step Pyramid and the 'bent' pyramid at Sakkar and Memphis on the west bank of the Nile. I was a member of the 512 Field Survey Company of the Royal Engineers, we produced and printed maps for the Army and the RAF. As a time served seven year apprentice I was proud to be a member of that select band in the Machine Section of the Company. We regularly maintained a seven day, three shift working whilst action prevailed in the Middle East theatre of war.

One of the culinary 'treats' of being on the night shift was the provision of rations from the cook house. These appetising treats came in the form of Australian tinned cheese and Australian tinned, smoked, rindless bacon. The cheese was akin to a likeable, mild, tasty Cheddar, excellent for sandwiches. The really big treat was "Welsh Rarebit" made from tinned cheese and tinned evaporated milk! Truly food fit for the Pharaohs! Our shift Corporal was accomplished and adept at conjuring up this memorable dish for eight or nine men. He used three primus stoves for the purpose and in addition gave us toast, tea and fried tomatoes. Seated at our well scrubbed trestle tables we tucked in with gusto. We used improvised tea bags, made with soaked linen paper we used for the maps!

Our camp was nearly five thousand years old believe it or not. The limestone caves were hewn out of the rock by ancient Egyptian craftsmen. This very same high quality limestone was used to clad and finish the exterior of the Giza pyramids, only a small amount of this cladding is left and can be seen on the peak of the largest pyramid of Cheops dating from many years BC. The remainder of this pale, creamy, buff coloured limestone, when polished and meticulously fitted, shone like alabaster in the golden sun and the cloudless ancient skies. It seems to me that, throughout the ages, men could not resist the temptation to use the area as a man made quarry but unfortunately over the years it has been ravaged. As I sit with my memories of nearly sixty years ago, I remember sitting in our unusual workplace, the five thousand year old caves eating our canned goodies, wonderful memories!"

Thank you Ken.

CHAPTER 5 - THINGS THAT GO BUMP IN THE NIGHT

The title of this chapter is not meant to indicate that you are going learn something about David Spain's nocturnal habits! For that, you should be grateful, believe me, his daytime habits are bad enough.

I like ghost stories because a) 'Spainy' can't take any photos and b) Investigating them often means squeezing into small spaces something 'DS' has great difficulty doing! I well remember his plaintiff cries when we visited Cuffley Camp, he had decided in his childlike way to hide in a hollow tree. The idea being to jump out on me, the jape went wrong when 'Spainy' got stuck.

No such luck on our visit to Chenies Manor though another bulky person did visit the Manor a few hundred years before us. Henry VIII and Anne Boleyn were entertained in the house by the first Earl of Bedford in 1534. Henry visited again in 1542 but he didn't bring Anne, she had already been despatched and King Hal was accompanied by Catherine Howard. Catherine was seven years younger than Henry's daughter Mary, and it is not surprising that she should find her elderly husband somewhat boring. Bearing in mind what had happened to Queen Anne, Catherine did a rather foolish thing, she began an affair with one Thomas Culpeper, who was an attendant to the King. When Tom accompanied the King and Catherine to Chenies, he took the opportunity to continue seeing Catherine. History tells us that the lovers were eventually punished on the block and that Catherine's ghost is said to haunt Hampton Court. As for the Chenies ghost, well it is said that the King himself can be heard dragging his gammy leg and moaning outside the bedroom where Catherine is said to have slept. The only groaning I heard was Mr Spain going on about food!

Just as a thought, remember the Thomas Culpeper we met at Wakehurst Place? The timing is right so maybe it was the very same Culpeper who tarried awhile with one of Henry's wives!

Queen Elizabeth often paid a visit to Chenies as well, though I am sure she acted in a manner more becoming to a monarch, after all she was known as the "Virgin Queen."During the Civil War a detachment of Roundheads were stationed at Chenies Manor and it is said that laughter can sometimes be heard, the suggestion being that it is the soldiers philandering with the servant girls. As if all this ghostly business were not enough, a headless man was seen walking in the gardens in the last century. In 1670 Lord William Russell was beheaded in London and his body brought to Chenies for burial. The headless man has not been sighted for sometime but doors are said to still open and close of their own accord.

Spring and late summer are good times to visit Chenies Manor, where the gardens are a revelation and there is plenty to see architecturally as well. 'Spainy' became fascinated with the Tudor privy for some unexplained reason. I was more interested in the story about Edward I arriving on a camel (to the Manor, not the privy).

Chenies Manor and Church, 2001

Chenies Manor gardens

As we drove away from Chenies Manor, "Spainy's" interest in loos became evident (I put it down to his public school education). "We could visit some more toilets," he mused. "We could also get arrested," I remarked. Not to be put off (or perhaps because he wasn't listening) he continued, "There was a man in St. Albans who turned a public toilet into a restaurant you know." Engaging first gear and trying to think of a way to change the subject I said, "I suppose the customers found that convenient." Still he ignored me, clearly he was in a little world of his own, a place where toilets were photogenic, a land of flushes rather than flashes! So it was going to be another of those days. As it turned out it wasn't, I managed to divert my friend's attention to other things, he took me to meet a friend of his.

An Exceptionally Pleasant Man

Francis Cory-Wright is a gentleman in the true sense of the word. His family links with Hertfordshire reach back to the times of the Norman Conquest! In Watton church, near Hertford there is a magnificent brass effigy of one Chevalier Philip de Petelot dating back to 1361, it is said to be the oldest military brass in the county. Princess Diana was one of Philip's descendants so Francis comes from a rather grand line! Another of his ancestors built Luton Hoo! We visited Francis at his wonderful home in the village of Little Gaddesden, Hertfordshire. He kindly showed us around the local area of the village including a house (parts of which were built in the 15th century) built on the site of John o' Gaddesden's birthplace. John (1280-1361) was the first physician to be appointed to a Royal Court and also was the first Englishman to write a textbook on medicine. Educated at Eton and Oxford, Francis Cory-Wright was commissioned into the 15th/19th The Kings Royal Hussars. He was wounded in action serving in World War Two. Travelling the world became very much part of his life; he served in the Foreign and Commonwealth Office with distinction. Expeditions, official and unofficial included Palestine and the Levant and Persia as well as Turkey, Mongolia, China, Peru and Chile along with a trip to locate the source of the Orantes. Archaeological Research is one of his passions and has fuelled his desire to collect and research oriental tribal rugs. A Fellow of the Zoological Society of London, Francis has an interest in deep sea fishing and wildlife studies in general. This turned out to be a very interesting visit to meet an exceptionally pleasant man. I was quite impressed with 'Spainys' behaviour, it only shows that he can do it when he tries (or as he would put it, that he is capable of adapting to any social occasion when put upon to do so!). Oh Yeah!

Francis Cory-Wright explaining the local history of Little Gaddesden to J.P.

Francis Cory-Wright outside John of Gaddesden's house, 1998

BACK TO THE GHOSTS!

It is Mr Spain's turn to tell a ghostly tale, I was surprised to learn that the ghost in question was not that of an overweight man clutching a camera and tripod, since the story comes from Abbots Langley, one of "Spainys" haunts! Mary Ann Treble was a servant at the vicarage of St Lawrence church, Abbots Langley before the First World War. Mary Ann's life at the vicarage is reported as being rather unhappy, it is claimed that she was ill treated by the vicar's wife. It is this lady, Mrs Parnall who is suspected of being responsible for the death of Mary Ann, we will probably never know the truth but we do know that Mary Ann was seen walking from her grave to the vicarage and even spotted in her former bedroom. Some years later the bedroom became damaged, nobody knew how, a builder was called. He told the occupants of the house that mending it would be pointless because Ann had died a terrible death in the room and the place would never be free of her. The ghost of Mary Ann Treble is still said to walk so, if you happen to be in Abbots Langley and spy a ghostly figure, and it doesn't offer to take your photograph, it's probably Mary Ann!

Mrs Parnall, the vicar's wife with boys from the local school

St. Lawrence Parish Church and Vicarage at Abbots Langley, 1993

CHAPTER 6 - MATTERS OF PASSION!

My choice of title for this chapter was quite deliberate, it was to get 'Spainy' going! "Passions," I told him, "A chapter on passions." His eyes developed a nervous tic, he fumbled with his zoom lens, stared into the distance, a vacant look on his face (even more vacant than usual). "Yes, well there was this rather pleasant blonde in Brazil," he hesitated. "Not that sort of passion, peoples hobbies and pastimes, things they are passionate about." I informed him. "Oh" was all he could muster and went back to playing with his tripod. There's a chap in Garston near Watford who grows orchids and he is passionate about them. Here I must tell you, I have no intention of including anyone in this chapter who has developed an interest to the anorak stage, simply people who have a hobby or a pastime they care about and who, are able to share it with others. John Cooke is such a man. So, before we take a look at the plants themselves, I thought I should treat you to some titbits of information. In order to do this small thing, I connected my computer to the Internet, about an hour later the printer ran out of ink and I was awash with information on orchids! So, it seems that a lot of people have a passion for orchids then. I won't go into too much detail, sufficient to say that Akeros Orkideer is an orchid vendor, my machine can't do those 'umlauts' and things they use in Germany, Sweden etc. but I am convinced Akeros Orkideer is to be found somewhere in Northern Europe. Then there is Joshua Hoiland whose website will regale you with "Photos of my orchids from my collection in Guatemala."

Pleurothallis lappago Luer

There is a Field Guide to the Orchids of Costa Rica, Craig Reavis's "Orchid Growing for the Horticulturally Challenged" that one will do 'Spainy' then, if anyone is horticulturally challenged David Spain is! He would happily pave his whole garden if Mrs Spain would allow. Incidentally, just a mention of Alice Spain, she is a lovely lady (you would have to be a saint to live with "DS"), but I have recently had cause for concern when I telephoned "Chez Spain" one evening and Mrs "S" answered. She informed me that the family were currently involved in a water fight in the garden. Fine, I had no problem with that, but she then went on to inform me that she was, at that very moment, in the act of removing her teeshirt! Now I am elderly, but still like to think that I am red blooded! I had to hang up. Later in the evening I spoke to the man himself, he told me that he was wet through and was about to remove his teeshirt! Sorry! Not the same effect at all! Anyway, back to the orchids. "Les Orchidophiles de Montreal", I am reliably informed have an interest in flowers rather than anything more unpleasant. Clearly there is a whole new world out there for me to discover, but not at the moment methinks. John Cooke in Garston near Watford in Hertfordshire will do for me as far orchids are concerned.

Since writing about listener John Cooke and his orchids, we were sorry to hear that he passed away recently.

John Cooke

Lycnoches Herrenissunam

Stanhopea Tigrina

Paphiopedolum Venustum

JENNY'S ORGANIC GARDEN

From John Cooke's home in Garston to Jenny Pates home in Dunton, Bedfordshire takes about an hour and it's worth it. Jenny is a remarkable lady who has a dream. Quite simply she wants to share her garden with the community. Jenny was born in the Bedfordshire village of Langford, "a long time ago". She attended Stratton School in Biggleswade and simply couldn't wait to leave "the flat county of Bedfordshire". Forsaking the county of her birth, Jenny went to university at Hull (frying pan into the fire then Jenny!). Jenny married and moved to Zambia to teach (and have babies!) for three years. Back in Silsoe, Bedfordshire, she enjoyed being a village housewife while her husband trained at the college in the village. At this time Jenny never gave any thought to having to search for a job, but circumstances changed and she moved to Reading. Circumstances changed again and Jenny discovered her present dwelling in Dunton, near Biggleswade. In truth, it was the garden that went with the Dunton house that caught her imagination. "I tried to renovate the cottage, do the garden, bring up three kids and work virtually full time. Guess which bit got really neglected?" Jenny's work has included Dunton playgroup for a couple of years, eight years with Bedfordshire's Special Adult Learning Programmes (basic education) and since 1983 a garden maintenance business and a couple of years at the Prospect Trust in Cambridgeshire working with their Garden Team. "I had to give up, the arthritis got the better of me, but I still raise a bit of money for them on Organic Open Gardens Weekends."

Gradually the idea dawned on Jenny that she should share her garden, it being too much for one family and so the Dunton Community Garden Scheme was born. It wasn't that easy of course and there is still much hard work to be done but, if I know our Jenny it will be completed. It's an organic garden, no chemicals are used and the group are always looking for new ideas. Open to people of all ages and ability the garden is a real haven, you will work for nothing but you will learn a lot as well. Jenny also runs courses, I particularly like the way willow is used to create living hedges and screens.

The garden is open to the public for the National Organic Gardening Weekends in June and August each year. On the open days there is music as well as craft stalls, plant and produce on sale, teas and lunches are also served. From April to October, Dunton is open to groups, members and individuals. Workshops are offered on various horticultural topics including organic gardening methods and living willow structures. The cottage offers a meeting room, quiet room and welcoming kitchen, which can be available by arrangement.

For information or details of opening times, telephone the Dunton Community Garden Group on: 01767 314599

Jenny Pates chatting with John Pilgrim in her garden at Dunton, Beds. 2001

A tour of Jenny's garden

JAVA JANE

Jane Oakley (known to her Internet friends as Java Jane) appears to have cracked the problem of not having enough hours in a day to get all she wants done. Jane owns her own company designing web sites and one of her customers describes her thus: "She is a nutter, and totally whacko, no interest in housework or any idea where the nail varnish is, which, I think makes her an excellent web designer". Who am I to disagree! So just how do Jane and her husband find time to breed butterflies? I don't know, but they do.

Jane explains: "To breed butterflies from ova to adult is an exciting hobby, and seeing a butterfly emerge from chrysalis stage is breathtaking. It is also educational for the children, who learn the life cycle and help to feed and care for the caterpillars and butterflies, our youngest can name nearly all the butterflies and caterpillars we see, and enjoys 'holding' the adults on her fingers and placing them on flowers or releasing them. To get this close to nature is magical."

How They Do It?

To begin with a cage is constructed of a wooden frame and base, then covered with fine muslin. The ova and very young larva are kept in plastic dishes (from take-aways) until they have either hatched or grown in Jane's garden or in pots. Most larval foodplants are what people consider to be weeds, Jane and her family prefer them to wild flowers for example, nettles, violets, plantains, wild grasses etc.

The caterpillars eat voraciously and the cages need daily cleaning to ensure healthy living (caterpillars poo too!). Some species grow quickly and are ready to pupate within a couple of weeks, such as the Peacocks and Small Tortoiseshells. They then amble to the top of the cage and hang from the roof on a fine silk thread, and spin a web of silk around themselves, turning into the chrysalis stage. The magical transformation from caterpillar to butterfly takes place and the adult butterfly emerges from its cocoon and puffs up the wings to dry out, ready for flight. Some common species, such as the Red Admiral or Peacock butterfly are released when they emerge. Jane says *"It is wonderful to have these beautiful insects on your hands and to watch them fly away. Others, such as the Silver Washed fritillary cannot feed, it is illegal to release butterflies that are not local to the area as this can mess up the natural system, and the foodplant required may grow in certain areas. These butterflies are fed with a solution of sugared water on cotton wool or nectar rich flowers."*

BEDFORD BUTTERFLY PARK

So it was only natural, after talking to Jane, that we should pay a visit to a young man who has gone a long way to realising his dream. Bedford Butterfly Park is the brainchild and fulfilment of ambition for its owner Andrew Green.

Born and raised in rural Lincolnshire, Andrew has always been fascinated with nature. With the open countryside as a playground he was quick to learn the names of wildflowers and the butterflies that visit them. His grandmother, whose father had been a keen naturalist, spurred on his interest. Andrew's great-grandfather was a renowned breeder of British moths and bred a new variety of the common Garden Tiger moth, called "petriburgensis petriburgensis". Being a modest man, rather than give this new variety his own name he preferred to name it after his home town of Peterborough! Andrew has recently discovered that most of Fred's collection has found its way to the Natural History Museum. Since opening Bedford Butterfly Park, Andrew has discovered that his great-great-grandmother was also a keen butterfly enthusiast.

Andrew went on to study Environmental Sciences at Hatfield before working in the environmental monitoring industry. However, his dream was always to set up and run his own Butterfly Park to show visitors the beauty of these creatures and help to educate them about the need for environmental conservation.

Andrew discovered the Bedford Butterfly Park site in 1996 and immediately realised its potential. A pattern of ridge and furrow on parts of the site indicated that the land had not been touched by modern farming practices. With the financial backing of his family, Andrew was able to purchase the site and work began on creating the Park. As the seasons passed it became apparent that Andrew's hunch about the land was correct and no fewer than sixty species of wildflower were discovered at the site. Working with the county ecologist, John Comont, Andrew has persuaded Bedfordshire County Council to give the site County Wildlife Site status in recognition of its importance to the county. The Park opened its doors to the public in 1999. The Park provides an excellent resource for local schools. In 2001, approximately, 2,500 school children aged four to nine visited the Park to learn about nature.

Bedford Butterfly Museum telephone: 01234 770770

Andrew Green talking to J.P. about his field untouched by modern farming methods

Interior of Bedford Butterfly Park

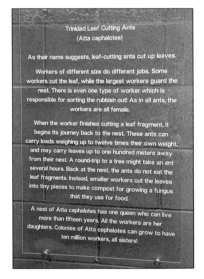

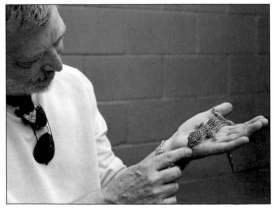

Some of the different varieties of specimens to be seen at the Butterfly Park

J.P. and owner Andrew Green get their goat!

Goats are only some of the animals to be seen at the park

CHAPTER 7 - TRAINS AND BOATS AND PLANES AND CARS!

"It's going to be a long day my friend", I advised my portly companion. 'Spainy' eased himself into the front passenger seat, stuffed his 'briefcase' (A Harrod's carrier bag) under the seat, adjusted his 'Save the Whales' tee shirt and replied "You know me John boy always up for it." Now, I have known David Spain for a few years and I have never, ever heard him employ such language! I decided to assume that he hadn't heard me correctly, so I repeated my warning "We've got a lot to do today." "Yes I heard you and I'm ready." This was going to be an interesting day! 'Spainy' up for it? It wasn't the right moment to ask him what he was up for, so I drove on. I admit that I was looking forward to seeing David's face (which, in itself only goes to show how my eyesight is failing) when we arrived at our first port of call.

Stondon in Bedfordshire is close to Henlow, Shefford and Henlow Camp. I'm sorry if I upset some of the residents of these villages, that's about it. Pleasant without being stunning that's Stondon. Except, for the Stondon Transport Museum. My companion had aptly displayed his readiness to be "Up for it" during the journey, he had dozed off! (It's not a pretty sight, he tends to dribble). "We're here, come on wake up, rise and shine, splice the mainbrace, sort out your tripod." He blinked two or three times, rubbed his eyes and took a look around, "Where are we? What do you mean, splice the mainbrace, we're in the middle of the countryside." "Never fear my friend, you will enjoy this, I promise." Slowly he focused on a sign at the roadside, Stondon Garden Centre, and said "I hate gardening." "I know you do but trust me." Now, quite apart from all the disparaging things I say about David, he does trust me, I can't think why, but he does. I think it must be his misplaced sense of honour, he can't believe that a Grammar School boy would let him down!

We pulled up in the car park and alighted, well I alighted 'Spainy' fell out of the car. "This is a place you are going to love," I told him and it was. John Saunders is a remarkable and extremely pleasant man. I took to him the very first time I met him and his Director and Curator Maureen Hird. They are my kind of people, hard working, a pleasant sense of humour and a feeling of what is right and wrong. There simply isn't enough space to tell you all things John has done in his life, he is over seventy years of age, going on twenty five! He leaves the day to day running of the museum to Maureen but can often be seen taking a stroll around his 'kingdom' of motor vehicles. Needless to say the moment he spied old motor vehicles, 'Spainy' began clicking away with his cameras. Leaving me some time to give you a rundown on the museum and John Saunders.

John began collecting classic cars over forty years ago, he ran out of space several times which is no surprise! He has been an engineering apprentice, worked in a drawing office, designed lightweight structures, was involved in restoration work on the famous Cardington Hangar doors as well as airframe design for De Havilland's. Not content with that, John set up his own company designing and manufacturing TV sets. He joined a company called Jekmol and ended up buying them out! Just happening to pick up a Royal Warrant on the way. While he was achieving the Royal Warrant and running Jekmol, John was also running a fleet (and building) cara cruisers (a type of vehicle capable of going on the road and the rivers). I guess John must have had some time on his hands because he began manufacturing greenhouses and lightweight garden buildings! In 1998 the Garden Centre at Stondon came on the market, it was close to home, so our John purchased it, his intention was to use some of the ground to house his ever growing number of vehicles. He allowed himself to be persuaded to try running the place as a garden centre but, when the field next door came up for sale, he bought it and built an area to house his vehicle collection. The museum has grown from strength to strength and is now the main attraction. I really admire John and Maureen, they never stop working. John is so active he makes me tired! Maureen (God bless her) keeps up with him seemingly without any effort at all. Just in case you might think that is the end of it, there is the small matter of Captain Cook's ship the 'Endeavour'! It's huge and you can take the kids aboard! Maureen researched Captain Cook and his journeys and then they built the replica ship at the Transport Museum! The cabins have the names of the original sailors who inhabited them on the doors, take the tour, take the kids, take your mum-in-law! Take a look at David Spain's and assistant Jackie's photographs

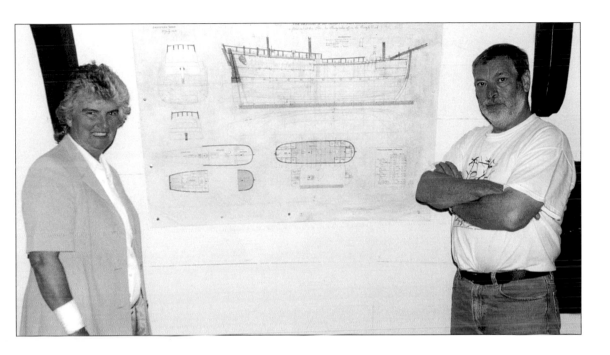

J.P. and Curator Maureen Hird showing the plans of Captain Cook's ship 'The Endeavour' being built at Stondon Transport Museum as a full size replica of the original ship

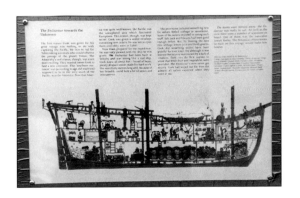

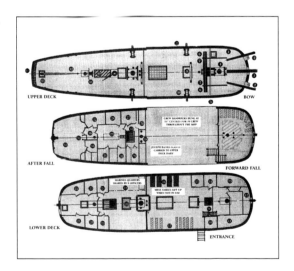

In 1768 Lieutenant James Cook, accompanied by Joseph Banks and Doctor Daniel Solander embarked on one of the most important voyages of discovery and navigation in natural science. Cook was an innovator, he fed his crew boiled cabbage, lemon juice and fresh vegetables to avoid them catching the dreaded scurvy. He was also the first to be able to calculate his ship's position using a complicated method of mathematics that had been developed in the early 1760's.

For information or details of opening times telephone: 01462 850339

SPAINY INDULGES HIMSELF

This is not for the faint hearted! And so, dear reader we come to the real reason that David Spain likes working with me. No, not because I make a mean bacon sandwich! Because, once in while I allow him to go gaga over trains, narrow boats and aeroplanes! I have never really been able to understand the hysteria with which the news that a steam train is about to make a Sunday afternoon trip is greeted. 'Spainy' goes all misty eyed, at the prospect, grabs his cameras, places his 1948 LMS guards cap on his head, pins his GWR (circa 1932) badge on the lapel of a stained drivers jacket (the one he would wear to work every day if Mrs Spain would allow it) and trundles off to wallow in nostalgia. So for those of you who, like 'Spainy,' mourn the passing of steam, then here are some of David's snaps from his archive collection, along with photos of the Buckinghamshire Railway Centre taken by his capable photography assistant Chloe.

For information or details of opening times telephone: 01296 655450

A flavour of the steam age to be seen at the Railway Centre, Quainton including a South African steam engine, a rebuilt railway station from Oxford as well as Thomas the Tank Engine and other attractions that can be seen on 'steam days'

The railway photos on the next three pages are dedicated to the work of the following great railway photographers and their families, who have allowed me to show their pictures over the years: C.R.L. Coles, H.C. Casserley, J. Habart, F.H. Stingemore and H.C. Doyle

A 'Black 5' double-headed with a 'Royal Scot' passing Berkhamsted

'Engineer Watford' at Watford Junction Sheds, 1928

A4 Lord Faringdon at Bushey Troughs, 1949

6235 City of Birmingham at Apsley, 1939

2-6-4T tank engine at Chorleywood, 1934

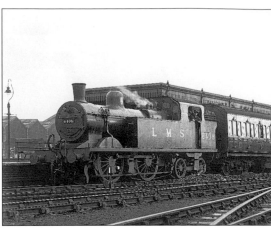

St. Albans branch train at Watford, 1936

Jubilee class steams out of Elstree Tunnel, 1962

'Blue Pullman' passing Mill Hill station, 1962

5735 'Comet' down express passing Rucklers Lane, Kings Langley in 1939

First Deltic Diesel on trials passing through Watford Junction, 1958 (now in Science Museum)

A 'young' Spainy with some of the saved steam engines at Barry Island scrap yard, Wales in 1976

More Trains and More! David Spain is ecstatic! Listen to this Dave! (I know it's a book but his reading is a bit questionable, so I will read this to him).

The opening of the London to Birmingham Railway in 1838 brought about the demise of the coaching trade almost overnight in the areas around what is now Milton Keynes. The old coaching inns at Stony and Fenny Stratford had to pick up the scraps from the rich man's table as it were, collecting passengers from the station to take them to the hotels. It is a fact that, if Wolverton had not become a railway centre, the area would have suffered even more. The half way point between London and Birmingham is Wolverton, so this was the point where the engines were changed. The original station in the town proved too small and a second station was constructed. This was also replaced when the main line was diverted to the locomotive and carriage works in 1881. The expansion resulted in the building of hundreds of railway workers houses but these went after just twenty years when the works themselves were expanded, so more housing was built to the south, but these also suffered in the 1960's. A printing works next to the railway works in Wolverton became a major employer of the wives and daughters of the railway workers; the brick front of Mc Corquodales built in 1884 was demolished in 1986. Much of the wall of the railway works survive.

I was lucky enough to be asked to officiate at the opening of the re-furbished open air swimming pool in Wolverton (2001). Local people worked very hard to save the pool and it is to their credit that, despite many setbacks, local children and families can once again enjoy the facility first opened in 1963. With the demise of the railways and the rise of nearby Milton Keynes it would have been understandable if Wolverton had lost its identity, but people still fight for their town. The pool is a monument to their enthusiasm.

My friend Jon Gaunt introduced me to his friends 'Barry the Boiler' and 'Half Man/Half Mac,' they accompanied me to the opening and 'Half Man' took these photographs as shown. 'Barry the Boiler' tells me that they are not as good as he could have done but what do I know, come to that what does Barry (or Half Man/Half Mac know?).

Two former coaching Inns at Stony Stratford, 2001

The opening of the re-furbished open air swimming pool in Wolverton, 2001

A Museum and More!

Milton Keynes has much to commend it, a modern, bustling city in the making. We should not, however forget that people have lived in the area for hundreds of years. Bill Griffiths and his colleagues at The Museum of Rural Life will certainly lose no time in reminding you. Situated on the site of a farm, the museum is just the place to take the kids, your grannie and granddad and (perhaps) the mother in law as well. 'Something for everyone' is often the claim made by places of interest and entertainment, in this case it is true. The farmyard has enough machinery to bring a glint to the eye of anyone who remembers the days when farmers had more than a couple of employees. A village street has been re-constructed inside to enable you get the flavour without experiencing the weather! Most of the shop fronts are genuine, having been removed from local sites and re-furbished, they include a pub! The kids have the chance to see what schooldays were like years ago when grannie was a child in the beautifully laid out school room. Everyone can wonder at the early days of the telephone, even make a call using proper pennies! The house itself is laid out as of days long ago and, as if all that were not enough.....lets take a look at the photos of Spainy and Chloe.

Telephone: 01908 316222

The Museum of Rural Life, Milton Keynes. Interiors show railway board room, school room and a pub frontage from a high street

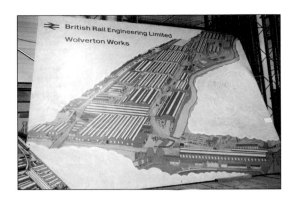

Photos showing farm implements, Wolverton Railway Works and L.N.W.R. steam engines

A Wolverton and Stony Stratford tram rests amongst other transport items from the local area

THE CANAL MUSEUM AT STOKE BRUERNE

David Spain behaved himself so well in Wolverton, I decided to reward him, "You almost deserve an ice cream, David," I told him. He grinned as only he can, "A '99' would be great." "No just an ice cream" I told him. You have to be careful with Public Schoolboys, bearing in mind the time they spent in Latin lessons reading the Kama Sutra. As it turned out I didn't have to satisfy my friend's sweet tooth, I simply took him to a place in Northamptonshire.

Stoke Bruerne is a must if you are, like 'Spainy' a nut about canals and narrow boats. "It is a very pretty village situated not far from Towcester in South Northamptonshire with a population of four hundred people. The Grand Union Canal runs straight through the village and it is especially interesting because of its locks and the tunnel. The boats have to be taken through the tunnel by means of a steam tug that goes from 5 am in the morning till 9pm at night, every two hours. The 'Towcester and Olney' Railway runs through the parish and has a station about half a mile from the village. The line is now only open for freight as passengers were not viable. The chief occupations of the local people are agricultural labourers, working in the Brickfield and on the Grand Union Canal. We have a full postal and telegraph office in the village, we have one delivery of letters and two outgoing posts. There is one public house, The Boat Inn. There is one blacksmith's shop and two shoemakers' shops and five grocers' shops. We have two woods in the villages, The Plain Wood and Stoke Park woods. The only drawback in Stoke Bruerne is that we are so short of clear pure water in the summer."

Stoke Bruerne Canal Museum housed in a former restored corn mill, 2001

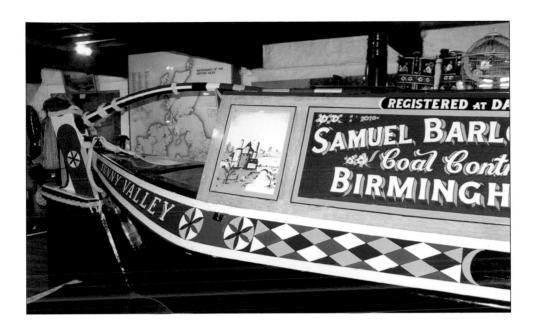

As I read the above from The Northamptonshire Village Book (published by Countryside Books, Newbury, Berkshire). 'Spainy' was at the wheel of his trusty motor vehicle, its the kind of car that has never seen better days, or at least if it has, then it is so far back in history that it can't recall them! He is a good driver, at least that's what he tells me, I can't comment because I close my eyes the moment I get into the car and don't open them again until we stop. We only stop at our destination, never in between, at least that's how it seems to me. When 'Spainy' drives, our journey is punctuated by expletives known only to public school boys, they are, I believe in Latin or at least that is what he tells me. So, onto the Stoke Bruerne Canal Museum. Over two hundred years of canal history is on display. Housed in a former, restored corn mill, the whole thing is greatly enhanced by the fact that outside the museum you have the real thing. The Grand Union Canal, locks and the Blisworth Tunnel. You can sign up for courses on narrowboat decoration, ropework and fendermaking. Take a cruise along the canal or take a walk along the towpath. There is also a shop selling souvenirs and a large collection of canal history books.

For details telephone: 01604 862229

View from the Museum window

Brian Collings, Site Manager

The Grand Union Canal at Stoke Bruerne, 2001

Chloe Fletcher a 'Tiller Girl'

The boat lift at Stoke Bruerne

Dutch barge passing through Kings Langley on its way to Milton Keynes, 1995

The lock at Dudswell, 1935

Horse-drawn wide boat nearing Lady Capel's Wharf, Watford, 1916

We left Stoke Bruerne with me agreeing with David, the romance of the canals and the boats is catching! "And now for some planes," he stated. I tripped on a branch left lying on the towpath by some thoughtful person, "Pardon!" He expertly placed a new roll of film into his 'Box Brownie' and with a sly smile (he knows how much I hate flying) said in a louder voice, "And now for some planes, don't worry, you haven't got to fly." It turns out that, among the many other subjects 'Spainy' has photographed, aeroplanes were once top of the list. "I used to take the occasional photo for Handley Page," he told me. For those who live or lived in the area of Radlett, Hertfordshire then the name 'Handley Page' will be familiar, indeed, for those with even a passing interest in aircraft, the name will mean a great deal. Frederick Handley Page (to be honest I always thought that the company name comprised of two surnames, one being Handley and the other Page, which only goes to show how much I know) was born in 1885 in Gloucestershire. He trained as an electrical engineer and became so enthralled with aviation that he began his own company in 1909. It was the first in this country for the purpose of Aeronautical Engineering. Under Handley Page's direction the first generation of British Heavy Bombers with multiple engines were produced. After World War One the great man designed the first real airliners and he ran them from the Company's aerodrome at Cricklewood to the continent. The Handley Page Hannibal series came along in the early thirties.

On the military side, never, since the day it was formed has the Royal Airforce been without an aircraft of Handley Page design on its active inventory. The 'Victor' bomber aircraft first flew in 1952. The aircraft's winning flight times in the Daily Mail Trans-Atlantic Air Races of 1969 bear witness to the designers' skills.

Another of Handley Page's aircraft served in virtually every war zone in the Second World War, remember Jack Bromfield's experience in the Halifax? Handley Page also helped to found Cranfield College, Bedfordshire. In 1990 the dedication of a memorial to Sir Frederick Handley Page and those who took part in the design, development and flying of his aircraft took place. It is situated at the entrance to the former airfield and works at Colney Street, near Radlett, Hertfordshire. As a young man I often marvelled at the size and power of the 'V' bombers as they took off from the airfield. Sir Frederick Handley Page was a truly remarkable man.

Memorial stone to Sir Frederick Handley Page

A newly built Handley Page 'Halifax' showing the technicians and staff at London Aircraft Production, Leavesden during the Second World War

A photo of a Handley Page 'Victor' Bomber taken in the 1960's

PHOTOS FROM THE 'OUT & ABOUT' AFTERNOON PROGRAMME

73

Chapter 8 - Curiosities, the Odd Murder and a Hermit

"Radlett said 'Spainy'. "Quite so" said I. "What do you know about Radlett?" he asked. "Well I know about Handley Page, we visited the former site to take some photos and then I found out more about Sir Handley Page, but you know I did, so why do you ask?" There's always an ulterior motive with Mr Spain and I rather suspected that he was about to advise me that he knew of a rather good café in Radlett. Not so! There was a murder and my friend was about to tell me all about it. It seems that he went to a 'Prep. School' in the area and also, years later, was involved in a book about Radlett and Aldenham written by Donald Wratten in 1989. So, bursting with knowledge he was about to tell me about a famous Radlett murder in Victorian times.

A Murderous Tale

It seems that at the time, the trial of the murderers created great interest across the land. John Thurtell, the son of a Mayor of Norwich was a gambler and promoter of illegal prizefights. William Weare another unsavoury character had, it was claimed cheated Thurtell out of some three hundred pounds at a game of cards. Thurtell called upon the services of one Joseph Hunt and together they planned to get Weare to agree to a shooting weekend to be held at the house of William Probert, another miscreant (amazing how many of these characters were abroad in Radlett! It wouldn't happen these days!). Anyway, as their gigs (two of them) approached the area where Oaks Close joins Gills Hill Lane, it is said that Thurtell drew a pistol and shot Weare then hurled him from the gig. He then jumped from the gig and beat Weare's head with the pistol and stabbed him. The body was dumped in a pond, removed and thrown into another pond. Thurtell had been observed by two alert farm labourers, who searched the area and found both the body and the murder weapons. The due process of law took over, the men were arrested and the subsequent trial caught the imagination of the public. The crime was re-lived in a dramatic form in London theatres and the provinces; people used the story to make their point about the immoral life led by gamblers. Joseph Hunt turned King's Evidence to avoid transportation to Australia, and Thurtell denied his part in the crime to the very day he was hanged at Hertford. Luminaries such as Sir Walter Scott, Charles Dickens, Thomas Carlyle and George Eliot all used references to the crime in their written work.

I listened as 'Spainy' related the story of the Radlett murder and wondered how I could top it (forgive the pun), decided that I couldn't so simply said "I used to cut the grass at Aldenham Church just down the road from Radlett." My companion didn't exactly scoff, public school boys don't scoff, they give you a condescending look that implies they have just found something nasty on the soul of their shoe! "So let's take a couple of photographs of the church," he said. What could I do? I followed, head bowed, 'Spainy' had scored a point!

I used to cut the grass at Aldenham churchyard. When my brother George began his garden maintenance business I was his only employee. In those days (here he goes again, I hear you say, off down memory lane!) garden maintenance as a way of making a living was quite new, as was the use of specialist machinery for the purpose. George had entered into a growing market, 'Allen' Scythes with a front bar of scissor like teeth were common; they were pretty hard work as well. Very soon, new machinery came along, the rotary cutter was a genuine innovation and it was one of these we used at Aldenham. Headstones, footstones and various other odd items hiding among the foot high grass would zip and fly like tracer bullets as we fought our way through, risking our eyesight and opening wounds on our forearms as branches slashed at us. Such a rural setting as Aldenham churchyard was not really the place for a youth of my age (and breeding!) to practise my Anglo Saxon, but I am ashamed to say that I did! At one stage the rotary mower broke down, so sweating profusely, I tried to re-start it, patiently I wound the rope start and tugged at it, I did this several times, nothing! Finally brother George appeared, admonished me and confidently took over, frantically he pulled at the rope start, nothing! George is some ten years older than me and, when you are just sixteen the age gap seems even larger, he had travelled the world on his own, seen and done a few things so Anglo-Saxon was nothing new to George. I stood there as my big brother gave a lesson in real swearing! Just as I was about to break into applause a voice broke our concentration, "Having trouble?" We looked up to see the head of a rather distinguished looking gent peering over a headstone. George explained our problem as the gent ambled towards us, businessman George noticed that said gent was carrying an old fashioned scythe. Fearing that another contractor was threatening our livelihood, my brother enquired who the gent was, to be honest he didn't really enquire, he asked gruffly, "And who are you?" The aforementioned gent explained that he was Lord Knutsford, one of the mainstays of the village church and just about everything else and that he was cutting the grass around the family graves! Strange to relate we did keep the contract for another couple of years.

Parts of Aldenham Church is built with 'Pudding Stone'. This rare rock, is peculiar to Hertfordshire; it was formed some eighty million years ago when an (earlier) Ice Age brought flints from the Chilterns, rounded them and dropped them over a beach where the sea came up to Elstree! It's a very hard rock but unfortunate in the sense that it looks just like bits of old concrete. It was never used much for building purposes but you can still find it in Radlett around Gills Hill and Aldenham Avenue.

Aldenham Church, 1989

While we were in the area of Radlett and Aldenham, 'Spainy' began to wax lyrical about the days he worked in the movies. I was tempted to ask him whether he was a body double for Moby Dick but he seemed so lost in his memories it would have been a shame to break his reverie. However he did dig out some photographs from the loft.

Spencer Tracey is seen here with some boys from Edgegrove Preparatory School, Aldenham during the making of 'Edward My Son' in 1949 (before 'Spainy' was born, so he didn't take this particular picture!).

Spencer Tracey and boys from Edgegrove School during the production of 'Edward My Son', 1949

And so, with David Spain still celebrating the fact that he knows more about Radlett and Aldenham than me, we got back into the car. I was desperate to regain my self- esteem as 'Mister Out and About' and then I remembered Mad Lucas! You don't seem to hear about hermits much these days, I suppose it's a bit difficult to find somewhere to live and be left alone! Anyway, back in the 1800's a certain James Lucas, a wealthy landowner seems to have found just the spot. Elmwood House, Redcoat's Green not far from Stevenage was the place.

Hermit of Redcoats public house

Redcoats Farmhouse Hotel near Hitchin

It's a sad story, but one which seems to have caught the imagination of Victorian England. Even the celebrated writer, Charles Dickens got in on the act. The Lucas family had owned estates in Ireland, Liverpool, Bedfordshire and Hertfordshire, they had also made a great deal of money through the slave trade and sugar. James Lucas never married, he had one brother and two sisters, not a great deal is known about his early life, but one can assume that, since he came from a wealthy family, James did not want for much in the way of material things. It seems that James contracted a rather nasty form of ringworm at some time in his childhood. His mother, Sarah remarked that "James was never quite the same after that". The boy suffered a great deal at the hands of the doctors whom his parents brought in to try to cure his illness. His school days were affected and young James often played truant. His parents tried to interest their son in the medical profession (a trifle odd when you bear in mind what the lad had suffered at the hands of doctors). The same thing happened when the church was suggested and there is little doubt that James' parents pandered to their son. His parents found it easier (less embarrassing probably) for James to remain at their Hertfordshire home when they were in London or elsewhere. James' father died at the age of fifty two and Sarah had to decide what to do with her family. James' conduct became more bizarre and Sarah sold the family home in London (bear in mind that officially James was now head of the family). Sarah called in the doctors and a Doctor Sutherland pronounced her son as being of unsound mind, an attendant was taken on to be with the lad night and day. The local inhabitants often watched as James Lucas engaged in his favourite sports in the grounds of Elmwood and although the boy grew to believe that he should be rightly in charge of things as the eldest son, it was brother George, a lawyer who visited and appeared to be in control. As time passed James ventured further abroad, locals would be surprised to see a half naked horseman bearing down on them! James fell in love with a girl he met whilst out riding. Lucas began to pester the girl, many people said that it was her marriage to a Reverend Hensley that caused James to become a recluse. The story becomes complicated because, records appear to show that James was thirty five when he confessed his love for the girl and that she could have only been about twelve years of age! His mother, Sarah died in October 1849 and James Lucas made some bizarre decisions. The undertaker called to remove Sarah's body, James refused to allow it to leave the house. Thirteen weeks later the undertaker was allowed to remove the coffin but only after Police intervention. One can only imagine exactly what was going on in poor demented James mind, he loved his mother, was obsessed with keeping her close to him and to have her taken away must have the final straw! Mad Lucas remained at Elmwood for twenty five years, he barricaded himself in to lead a life of seclusion. Effectively he made himself a prisoner in his own kitchen, complete with iron bars. He became wasted and slovenly, his hair grew waist length and mostly he sat with an old blanket around his shoulders. James did speak to people, always with his gun at side and never allowing them inside his home-made prison, we will never know the complete truth about Mad Lucas.

Richard Whitmore has written the full story of 'Mad Lucas', it is well worth a read.

Having related the story of Mad Lucas to 'Spainy' we left Redcoat's Green and drove across to another Hertfordshire village, well Northchurch is more of a town these days (no offence to the locals). There, in the churchyard you will find the grave of 'Peter the Wildboy'.

"Peter, the wild man from Hanover. Whoever will bring him to Mr. Fenn, at Berkhampstead, Hertfordshire, shall be paid for their trouble." These are words inscribed upon the collar worn by the so called 'Wild Man'. Discovered practically naked in woods near Hanover in 1725 the boy's plight caught the imagination of King George I who had him brought to England. One assumes that George and his friends became bored with the lad because he ended his days in Berkhamsted. He was placed in the charge of a farmer named Fenn, but Peter was apt to wander off, hence the collar and its inscription. He died in 1785 at around seventy two years of age, there is a memorial brass in St. Mary's, Northchurch placed there by the government of the day.

The grave at Northchurch and a drawing of Peter the Wildboy who was brought over by King George I in 1725 from Hanover, Germany

The rear of Hunton Park Management College (formerly Hazelwood House), 1996

"I know a place where blue movies were made." Now there's a statement you can't ignore! We had just climbed back into the car and I was intending to make my way back home, naturally, I was going to drop 'Spainy' off first or we didn't have enough food to feed him for a night! I paused for just a moment before I answered, (well you would, wouldn't you?). Have you got a friend who knows where blue movies were made? So off we went to Hunton Bridge, it wasn't out of our way, 'Spainy' lives nearby.

We were soon driving towards a rather grand looking mansion situated on the edge of Hunton Bridge. Mr Spain was able to explain the history of the place but before that he explained that the film 'Raging Moon' was filmed in the area, "That wasn't a blue movie" I told him, he sighed as only a public schoolboy can, you know with that air of superiority honed by beating oneself with birch twigs and learning Latin, "That comes later."

'Hazelwood', now called 'Hunton Park' was the brainchild of Henry Botham. In 1812 he purchased the land and set about achieving his aim of building a fine mansion. Over the years the house has been home to several well to do people. Lord Rokeby fought as a sixteen year old at the Battle of Waterloo, by the time he fought at Sebastopol he had risen to the rank of Major General. Rokeby retired to Hazelwood and much improved the estate. The Rev. Gladstone lived at Hazelwood, he was related to the Prime Minister of the same name. The house was destroyed by fire around 1907 and the Reverend received ten thousand pounds from his insurance company; when you think that the house is owned these days by the Prudential it's nice to know that insurance works!

Violet Cressy - Marcks was one of the first female explorers, she lived at Hazelwood from 1930. Employed by the Daily Express, she was their special war correspondent. Violet became the first English person to gain an interview with Mao Tse Tung in China.

Another well-known resident of Hazelwood was Emperor Haile Selassie of Ethiopia, he lived there secretly after the Italians invaded his homeland during World War Two. Some of the land surrounding the house became part of Leavesden airfield and was used during the Second World War for aircraft manufacture by London Aircraft Production who built Mosquitoes and Halifax Bombers. Today, as I have mentioned, the house is owned and used by the Prudential as a corporate training and conference centre for the use of both the company itself and outside businesses. The men from the 'Pru' have restored the magnificent gardens and continue to work to bring them back to their former glory. "That's all very interesting 'Spainy' but what about the blue movies", "ah, I thought you had forgotten, follow me."

Tucked away behind Hazelwood is a rather pleasant house. When we visited it was where Morgan cars from all over Europe were refurbished. Bob Harper, the owner of the business, showed me six or seven Morgan cars. He explained how they were refurbished and offered to take me for a spin. I should have declined but I didn't, I squeezed into a car, switched on my tape recorder and closed my eyes! We sped along the lane leading to Hazelwood with me doing my very best to be Murray Walker. On our return my rotund photographer friend had a supercilious grin on his face, "So how was it?" he asked. I declined to comment choosing instead to remind him that this visit was supposed to be all about blue movies. " Follow me" he said and ambled off into the garden. "See that opening there," he asked, pointing towards what appeared to be the entrance to a tunnel. "I do, but you aren't going to tell me they made a blue movie down there are you?" As it turned out, he wasn't but the cavern we entered was nevertheless interesting, probably something to do with mining flint. Halfway down the tunnel 'Spainy' decided that he couldn't force his bulky body any further. His voice echoed along the tunnel, "If you get out safely I will tell you about the blue movies." Safely back above ground I brushed myself down. "Very interesting, now what about the movies," he waved his arm expansively encompassing the whole of the garden, "This is where it was made." I asked him how he knew all this and it appears that it is quite true. Back in the fifties when blue movies were not really blue someone used the garden to film various maidens and chaps wandering about making fools of themselves without any clothes. Muttering something about, "They were probably public school boys." I returned to the car and drove Mr Spain home.

Bob Harper about to give J.P. a 'thrill' by taking him out for a ride in his red Morgan

I couldn't think of anything to upstage "Spainy's" blue movie story so I arranged to lose him! Near Shefford in Bedfordshire lives a man who could help me. John Brindle is a chap who knows his own mind, he grew apples but didn't like the idea of what chemical spraying would do to the environment. He changed his approach to apple growing but people didn't purchase them! Nothing daunted Mr Brindle chopped some of the trees down and constructed a maze. It now takes a week to trim the Golden Leylandii trees that form the maze. Oh yes! John also makes boomerangs, speaking of things that keep coming back, here are a couple of photographs taken by a certain Mr Spain!

It's easy to miss the entrance to the maze so take it slowly and drive south east of Shefford, about halfway towards the roundabout just where the A600 meets the A507. It's on your right, at least the notice telling you where it is, is!

John Brindle, the boomerang man interviewed by J.P., 2001

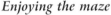
Enjoying the maze

In 1885, a family business began in the village of Holme, close to the Bedfordshire town of Biggleswade. It is now an international business and still owned by the Jordan family. I was fortunate enough to interview two of the Jordan family at the mill a few years ago. John Jordan is a real character, he loves flying and it has got him into a few scrapes in his time. John and his lovely wife have lived in the house beside the mill since the 1940's. It was always going to be a life with the family business for John, well not really! As far as I can make out and from what he tells me, John had other things on his mind from a very early age. This is not to say that the Jordans' business was going to take second place, just that young John had things to do before he settled down. The trouble is, he hasn't settled down yet! John flew over two hundred different Spitfires in World War Two, yes over two hundred! It was his job to deliver the aircraft. Young Jordan discovered a love for flying early in his life, just across the fields from Holme stands Shuttleworth the former home of Richard Shuttleworth, the man who won the first British Grand Prix and took to the air in those wonderful early flying machines. As a young man John Jordan would gaze into the sky in wonder as Shuttleworth took to the air, one day he sitting on a farm gate watching Shuttleworth prepare to take off for a flight. "He beckoned to me and I assumed he was offering to take me up for a spin," John told me, "That was it! I wanted to be a flyer." As far as I can tell, you don't get in the way of Mr Jordan senior when he makes up his mind, so a flyer he became. Much later in life John was asked to fly over Mount Everest, well you do don't you? "I didn't quite make it, the plane wouldn't make the height but I did get frostbite," he says in quite a matter of fact manner. Appearances in several films followed, he was a German Baron in the movie 'Biggles'. His son, Bill informs me that John still has the leather coat worn by the 'Baron' in the film. Today Jordan's is a highly successful international company, making breakfast cereals and breakfast bars. The family still run the business and are proud of their local Bedfordshire roots. When you visit the area, and you should it is an idyllic spot, take a look at the 'Jesus Bust' a statue said to have been made by an Italian prisoner of war who was working in the mill at the time. The statue is opposite the mill on the banks of the river. There's a shop where you can pick up some rather pleasant gifts and also items of food manufactured by Jordans. Pay a visit to the village of Broom and Holme Mill there is a great pub standing on the village green! Just perfect for a Sunday afternoon drive.

Photos showing John Jordan (now and then) and his family mill

'Jesus bust' statue made by an Italian POW who worked at Jordan's mill

"Little people," said 'Spainy'. "Overweight people," I answered suspiciously, remembering his previous escapades photographing toilets. "They wouldn't get in," he said. Wishing that Merchant Taylors' school had taught my friend to begin at the beginning and continue from there, I sighed inwardly and prepared myself for a long, drawn out conversation. A conversation built around the techniques I had read about in books, you know the sort of thing, you place the suspect in a chair, shine a bright light in their eyes, clench your fists and bellow things like, "OK brain I know you're in there somewhere, come on Spain spill the beans or it will be the worst for you." By the time we had reached the café it had become clear that Mr Spain was suggesting we visit the Model Village at Beaconsfield, quite why he hadn't simply said, "Why don't we go to Bekonscot?" I don't know, but there you are it's just one of the reasons we take a year to put a book together, there are other reasons but they have to do with David Spain's habits, and believe me you don't want to know!

Beaconsfield or 'Beckensfield' as the locals prefer to call it, is said to have got its name from Bekenesfeld which is, not surprisingly thought to mean 'field by a beacon' all right so far it's not too exciting I know but it gets better. The present Parish Church stands on a site where a wooden church stood some nine hundred years ago. The thirteenth century saw a royal grant obtained to hold a market in the town. The four 'ends' to be found in the town, London, Windsor, Wycombe and Aylesbury form the cross-roads. All this dates back to the time when the town became part of an endowment to Burnham Abbey and the Abbey received fees from the market and indeed, the annual May Fair (still held today). After the dissolution of the Abbey the town and the area surrounding it were divided into three estates, Hall Barn, Gregories and Wilton Park.

Hall Barn was once the home of the poet Edmund Waller, he also played a prominent part in the Civil War. He was tried for treason and managed to escape the death penalty, receiving instead a heavy fine and an invitation to live abroad, I believe they called exile! He was allowed to return home in time and he built the present house in around 1675.

Gregories (in my vocabulary a Gregory means cheque, Gregory Peck, cheque, get it?). Edmund Burke extended Gregories when ownership passed to him in 1768. Burke entertained several notables of the day at his home, Sir Joshua Reynolds, Oliver Goldsmith, Garrick and Dr. Johnson being among those who passed through the portals. Burke is buried in St. Mary's Church, before he died he re-named the house 'Butlers Court'. I don't know why, perhaps he had a penchant for butlers.

Wilton Park was built in the early part of the eighteenth century and purchased in 1779 by one, Josias Du Pre, he had formerly been Governor of Madras, India. There is a monument to Josias in St. Mary's. The War Office took over Wilton Park during World War Two and used it as an interrogation centre for senior prisoners of war. Rudolf Hess was among those who were 'visitors'. It was demolished in 1967 to make way for some military buildings. Pity really it would have been an ideal place to try to get some sense out of 'Spainy'!

Bekonscot the model village was the real reason for our visit. I hadn't been there since I was knee high to a grasshopper (and that, believe me, is a long time ago). It really is a wonderland for kids and adults alike, I had quite forgotten just how much fun there is to be had wandering like Gulliver through the village. Naturally, 'Spainy' was much too large to be allowed in, I had to explain it to him afterwards. He did manage to lean over the fence to take a few photographs though, with the help of his captivating assistant Chloe!

An English village in miniature at Bekonscot, Beaconsfield, Bucks

Bekonscot began as a hobby for a London accountant. Roland Callingham bought a field in the 1920's, he dug a pond and built a few model houses, a friend, James Shilcock added a model railway. Mr Callingham lived in Beaconsfield and Mr Shillcock in Ascot, so they called their village 'Bekonscot', simple really! The village was opened to the public in 1929, no charge was made, but the owners relied upon the public to place money in a collection box. In 1932 the Bekonscot Model Railway and General Charitable Association was set up to administer the village and distribute any money left over from the running costs to charity. There has always been a connection with the Church Army and in 1978 a company was started and was managed by them. Over a million pounds (at today's prices, over three million) has been distributed to charity. Roland Callingham never intended that his village should be run as a profit making business, he built it for pleasure, and indeed it does bring pleasure to thousands of people each year. Enid Blyton lived in Beaconsfield and her house 'Green Hedges' is depicted in the model village. Blyton also wrote a story about two children who visit Bekonscot. So pay a visit to this miniature wonderland, amble through six tiny villages, visit the zoo, watch a village cricket match or even listen to the organ music from the steam organ at the village fair, and imagine David Spain jumping up and down because Bekonscot has a model railway and he is too large to be allowed in!

Telephone: 01494 672919 for details on Bekonscot Model Village

Views of Bekonscot Model Village taken in the Summer of 2001

On our way to Beaconsfield we had passed the sign for Denham, a village I had intended to visit for sometime. I have always been fascinated by the movies and knew that several well known actors had made their homes in Denham over the years. So, on the way back from Beaconsfield we took a detour. Denham is, and I quote from "Buckinghamshire" (Roscoe, London Methuen Ltd, 1935): "Remarkable for its many examples, in and near, of medieval domestic architecture. It is a delightful old-world village with a single street of picturesque houses, large elm trees, pleasant meadows and little streams, among which it lies." So old Roscoe liked Denham you may assume, so did we, even if it has changed a little since 1935.

Oswald Moseley lived in the village for a while, though nobody cares to talk about it very much and who can blame them? I only remember the name because I heard people talk about him and I have seen film footage on television. I was surprised to learn that, in his time Moseley was a member of both the Labour and Conservative parties. In 1931 Moseley founded the New Party, which he led until his internment during the Second World War. Moseley was denounced in 1946 when it became known that Italy had funded his pre-war efforts to establish fascism in the UK; in 1948 he resumed his fascist propaganda. His second wife is buried in the church graveyard at Denham.

A much more entertaining story from the village is that of Alexander Korda. Flamboyant is probably the best way to describe Korda's life style, with his chauffeur driven Rolls Royce and a suite at 'The Savoy', he certainly impressed city banker Leopold Sutro. Korda was determined to start his own film studios, he had the talent and the enthusiasm all he needed was the money. Enter stage right, Mr Sutro, along with Kordas two brothers, Vincent and Zoli, they formed London Film Productions. Their first film was The Private Life Of Henry The VIII with Charles Laughton as the King. The script was written by Lajos Biro who had worked with Korda in Budapest, but there was bit of a problem! Biro had almost no knowledge of English and Vincent spoke no English at all! Difficulties with cash flow were of a daily concern to the Kordas but they persevered, the film was made and, the rest is history. The name of Korda stands along with the best of them in the annals of British film making and it all began in Denham.

Entrance to Denham Village

Views of Denham Village, 2001

Roman remains have been found in Denham and it is quite clear that the area was settled in Saxon times. Denham Court is a particularly fine house as is Denham Place, the gardens at Denham Place were landscaped by none other than 'Capability' Brown.

We are very grateful to Eric Evans, church yard caretaker, grave digger and gardener at Denham Church for helping us with his expert knowledge of the local area.

Now for another Denham success story, one concerning ingenuity and bravery and which has resulted in the saving of many lives, world-wide.

The Martin Baker Company is a very special one. During World War II the German Luftwaffe experimented with some minor success, with ejector seats for its pilots. After the war Martin Baker took up the challenge to develop a practical escape system for aircraft pilots. Strange to relate, that in the village of Potton, Bedfordshire,

I met a man who worked as a test pilot on ejector seats!

Usually, you find that ordinary people who carry out brave tasks are modest and somewhat retiring and so it was when I visited Peter Page at his home. My intention was to spend about half an hour with Peter, I ended staying well over an hour. I left with the feeling that some official recognition should be given to Peter for his bravery. Peter volunteered for the Parachute Regiment during the World War II. He completed his training and made twenty-seven jumps from aircraft during the war years. Peter dismisses his wartime experiences as something that simply happened and insists that any young man would have done the same thing. I simply cannot imagine what it would be like to wait in an open door of an aircraft, in flight, at night, knowing that the enemy was waiting below. When I asked Peter to recall his feelings in a combat situation he shrugged and smiled and then told me that in East Africa the Germans were conspicuous by their absence when the Paras landed; in fact when the soldiers tried to collect their parachutes they found that the local Arabs had got there before them.

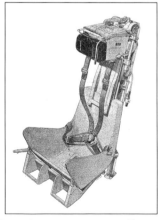

Pictures showing Peter Page, the first ejector seat test pilot with view of ejector seat and test rig

After the war Peter Page wanted to make his living within the aircraft industry and found himself working for the Martin Baker Company, little did he know what life had in store for him! Peter volunteered to test the company's ejector seats. Strapped to a seat on a one hundred and ten foot metal tower, Peter was launched vertically by pulling a kind of flap over his head! I saw film of the tests and, with freeze frame technique, it was easy to spot a smiling Peter Page about to launch himself up the tower! The film also shows several Royal Airforce types, hands in pockets, laughing and joking with Peter prior to the test. Following on from the initial test runs, Peter made a successful ejection from an airborne Meteor jet and reported that the seat worked well. It was, however, his second attempt that was to change Peter's life. At a height of eight thousand feet and travelling at over four hundred miles an hour, Peter fired the mechanism and the seat exploded upwards and out of the aircraft. All seemed to go well, the parachute fixed to the seat opened but Peters legs had been forced apart by the blast and he had a quick decision to make. Quite how you make a decision when you are tumbling towards earth, I'm not sure, Peter decided to stay with the seat, he hit the runway and lay on the ground, unable to gain his breath and sure that he was paralysed. He was rushed to hospital in Oxford where a specialist (luckily) realised that Peter's back was broken. He was placed in sandbags, six months later the plaster was removed. Unable to continue his work with Martin Baker, Peter Page made his way through life safe in the knowledge that he may have made flying safer for the pilots of the future. Martin Baker ejector seats have saved the lives of over ten thousand fliers, Peter has received many letters over the years, one of his favourites is from Flight Lt. Peters whose life was saved in the Gulf War. To this day The Martin Baker Company is the only manufacturer of aircraft ejector seats in the world. We found the inventor's grave in Denham churchyard and on it is inscribed an ejector seat.

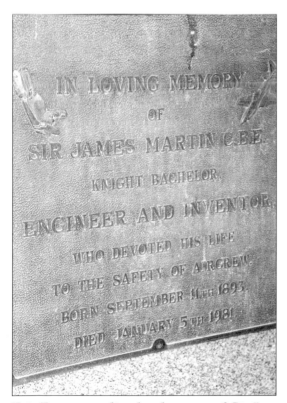

Eric Evans standing by the grave of Sir James Martin, inventor of the aircraft ejector seat

Chapter 9 - A 'B' and an 'O'!

It was a decidedly chilly morning when 'Spainy' arrived at the café. Boldly he pushed the door open, smiled broadly and tripped over the step! Everyone else laughed, I (being a right old softie', helped him up and offered to buy him breakfast). "Oh thank you very much, I'm not that hungry to be honest so I'll just have the full breakfast with extra toast. What seemed like minutes later (it must have been more, even 'Spainy' can't eat that fast), he clapped his hands and wiped his chin, and asked, "Where are we off to then?" "A 'B' and an 'O' I replied. He blinked, then looked around the café, "Some of them are all right." "No the places we are going to visit, one begins with the letter 'B' and the other with an O.' I was tempted to add, "And there's a third, you berk," but didn't.

'B' For Baldock

Baldock was abandoned, or so it seems in the fifteenth century, perhaps a family of Spain's moved in and other, more normal people chose to move out, who knows? Anyway we decided to take a look. I well recall my first visit to Baldock, it was in the sixties, when coaches (motor driven) still stopped there on their way north from London. It was to be my first visit to Scotland and the only thing I remember about the journey was that the chap sitting next to me took off his shoes! So maybe it was with some not so good memories that I returned to this town which was a coaching stop long before I meandered my way north with my nose being assaulted! Baldock was to the Knights Templar around 1250 and took its name from the old French word for Baghdad! Strange to relate, the most impressive frontage is that of the local Tesco store, which has something to do with the fact that the building used to be the home of a hosiery firm; it was also a film studio for a while. Some evidence that the Romans visited has been found. In medieval times the town lay within the manor of Weston (the village where Busbies for the Queens soldiers were manufactured but that's another story). The church of St Mary merits a visit and the surrounding villages will serve to make a day trip to the area worthwhile. Older people remember that before the First World War there was only one local employer of any note, the brewery. A steam dray was used to deliver beer further afield. It was in the 1920's that a new employer arrived in the town. A stocking factory is hardly what you would have expected but a stocking factory it was. Perhaps this was the time when Baldock was to receive a new import of accents and culture. Workers from Nottinghamshire and Leicestershire arrived to work at the Bonsor factory. Strange to tell, it was one of my regular listeners known as 'Lady Elizabeth of Walkern' whose legs once adorned the advertising boards across the land! Show a leg 'Spainy', take some photos!

Baldock High Street, 2001

Views of Baldock shops, St. Mary's Church and the impressive frontage of Tesco superstore, 2001

THE OVALTINE FACTORY IS GOING!

"It's all coming to an end you know", we were driving back from Baldock and I was a little tired but I responded because, sometimes you have to humour him. "What's coming to an end?" I asked, expecting him to inform me that he had experienced a dream involving an invasion from Mars, little green men, and ending with him walking the streets of Watford sporting a sandwich board advising the population that we were all doomed. You never can never tell with 'Spainy', he is prone to odd dreams, most of them I cannot, for reasons of propriety relate. "Ovaltine," he said. Now, I have long been an admirer of the malt based drink that helps you to spend a pleasant night in bed (careful!) and so, I was somewhat surprised to hear that I was no longer going to be able to burn the milk in the saucepan in an effort to gain a good night's sleep. "What exactly are you going on about 'Spainy'. "Ovaltine are leaving us." It seems that the company are off to pastures new which is a shame, but it does give us the opportunity to take a look at Ovaltine in our area.

First some facts, it was in the year of 1865 that a Swiss gent by the name of Dr. George Wander became aware of the value of barley malt in our diet. He promptly launched Ovaltine, what a clever fellow, don't you just wish that you could have thought of something like that? (personally, I dislike the man and Richard Branson, Chris Evans and all those other highly successful people who got there before I did). It's all right, I've calmed down now, so it's back to George Wander and his son. Albert Wander who took over from his dad and 'twas he who developed markets abroad. Kings Langley in Hertfordshire became the place of manufacture. The factory was built in 1912 and manufacturing started in 1913. Between 1924 and 1929 the factory was expanded. Wander Limited was on its way!

In 1929 Wander purchased Numbers Farm, Kings Langley and Parsonage Farm at Abbots Langley. The farms produced eggs, barley, milk and malt for Ovaltine. Wander also had their own fleet of narrow boats on the Grand Union Canal. The Ovaltine Farms at Kings Langley and Abbots Langley were a fine sight when I was lad, with thatched roofs and pristine settings. At its height the Ovaltine factory was producing an unbelievable 175,000,000 sachets per year! Sleep on that!

Aerial views of the Ovaltine Factory, Kings Langley taken in the late 1940's

Views of the Ovaltine Factory, Model Poultry and Dairy Farms

The Morecambe and Wise show in 1960's

Susie Spain (aged 3) by the renovated Ovaltine narrowboat 'Albert'

CHAPTER 10 - GO ON! INDULGE YOURSELF, I'M GOING TO

The question of family history comes up time and time again on my radio programme. More people seem to be interested in their past than ever before. So why not have a go? That's how you might indulge yourself, now it's time for me to do the same. My brother Bill has been researching the Pilgrim family history for two or three years. The trouble with Bill is, he's a perfectionist and only gives me scraps of information. He has produced a first draft of his history of the Pilgrims and, although so far, he has not discovered too many skeletons in the cupboard or any rich or famous Pilgrims, we (that's the rest of us Pilgrims) live in hope. Bill's history has been put together in a fascinating way, he has researched the times our forefathers lived and the areas they inhabited, this gives a real flavour of the times when my great granddad was doing his best to bring up his family etc.

I was born in the upstairs front room of number fourteen Richmond Way, Croxley Green, Hertfordshire in the year of our Lord 1942 BS, that's before Spain (He never misses the chance to remind me that he is younger than me and I never miss the chance to tell him that, I look younger than him). Back to my mum and dad, Arthur George Pilgrim probably lied about his age when he married Ivy Dorothy Stanton. Vanity I expect, though I can't be sure. Mum always told us that her family thought that 'AG' as he was known to friends and enemies alike, was a 'good catch', it's also true that she told us for the rest of life that she didn't like him very much! As a youngster, I agreed with mum, but with hindsight (and isn't that a wonderful thing!), I don't think that she really disliked the 'old man' (he hated being called that so, as kids we did it all the more, horrible little buggers!). On the subject of dad's age and his vanity, mum also told us that everyone thought that he was a sort of Rudolf Valentino, very well dressed in his double breasted suit, hair slicked back and all that. Before I came into the world three other little Pilgrims had been delivered to 'AG' and Ivy Dorothy. June was the first, Bill (I won't tell you his full name, he still hates it) the second and then another Arthur George, two more sisters followed me, Linda and Susan (the bane of my young life as I recall). I was born into an odd sort of household really, at least it seems that way to me now. Mum and Dad fought, mostly verbally, though fisticuffs did come into the relationship at times. I don't think that my arrival was to blame, my older siblings tell me that things were pretty much the same for them as they grew up, first in Acton, London and latterly in the verdant countryside of Croxley Green. So, let us examine this household (as Lloyd Grossman would say). Remember this explanation is coloured with hindsight and the experience of life (where things are never black and white). I hate arguments and rows and I particularly hate violence, that is strange when you consider that, during my own working life I have placed myself in some pretty desperate situations, maybe I was trying to prove myself, I don't know. I put my dislike of violence down to the shouting matches mum and dad indulged in. As a kid I blamed dad, as a young adult, I blamed mum, as a man I find it difficult to apportion blame. They were my mum and dad and I loved them, still do. Times were hard during their early married life, nothing outstanding there, things were tight for ordinary working people.

'AG' grasped his opportunity when it arrived, he was declared unable to go into the forces during the Second World War, an accident had seen to that, don't ask me exactly what was the matter with dad, I can't tell you, I do know that, in later life he became almost crippled and drove one of those horrible little fibre glass invalid carriages (he thought it funny so don't feel sorry for him, he would have hated that). Where was I? Oh yes the war, dad was working for H.J. Heinz the baked beans people at the time and they took over a large house in Croxley Green for the duration. I know very little of the 'ins and outs' of all this you understand, only what I have gleaned over the years. So dad was asked to move into Hertfordshire to take over 'The Grange' as a sort of caretaker cum gardener. He rented the house in Richmond Way, probably intending to move back to London after the war. 'AG' was a survivor all right and what's more, he saw to it that his family wanted for very little. Brothers and sister assure me that 'the old man' looked after the family as well as he jolly well could (come to think of it, for jolly insert bloody, dad would not have used jolly, nor bloody either but I am too well mannered!). June, the eldest was very much mum's right hand girl, Bill and 'AG' the younger plagued her and mum and, it seems to me, most of Croxley Green, they spent their war dodging school, scrumping and generally being boys. My own earliest memories include driving the horse and cart for the local baker when I should have been at school, at the time mum was in hospital with thrombosis, she nearly died and, years later related an 'out of body experience'. She insisted that she found herself in a black tunnel, as if she were drowning, she told me that she willed herself to clamber out of the tunnel, knowing my mum, she probably did, I never knew another person with so much willpower. I grew out of driving the bakers cart but never out of hating school. Brother Bill joined the Royal Air Force and applied for a posting in Egypt (his love of all things Egyptian came from, I know not where). Shame really, he spent five years in the RAF, several of them in Egypt but never got to see the pyramids! George had one of several fallouts with dad and emigrated to Australia at the age of seventeen. Even this was not plain sailing, in order to outflank 'AG' senior, George got the local vicar and policeman to sign his immigration papers. I well remember the day he departed, a callow youth of seventeen or so, mum had squeezed all his worldly belongings into one bag and I was packed off to school (yes, I did go that day) with tears in my eyes, my hero was leaving home and my dad was to blame. That night 'AG' senior arrived home and sat down for his tea (I seem to be making dad out to be a horror, to me then he was, but not later). The poor old bugger was holding down two jobs at the time and must have been completely knackered. "So where is he then?" dad asked, meaning George, remember they had been involved in a vendetta for some time. Mum and June burst into tears, "He's gone to Australia" said mum, or words to that effect. 'AG' never flinched, he continued to eat his meal. The next day dad got up and went to work, that evening, he told us that he was going to have the boat stopped and George sent home, more tears and recriminations from mum and June and of course, young John joined in! What a disaster! What a calamity! How would the drama end? The boat made its way to Australia and George was gone for five years. June married her childhood sweetheart Joe and Bill returned from Egypt (having missed George as his boat sailed through the Suez Canal!) and as for me? Well I continued to hate school, steer clear of dad whenever I could, drove June mad and nicked my little sisters savings stamps! And then I met Bill the Greengrocer! In those days nearly everything you required to sustain life was delivered to your door. Bertie Brandon (a mate of dad's) had a little van and he would deliver all sorts of goodies, if so required. Milk came from the 'Hygienic Diaries' (two rounds, both horse and cart, both milkman named Fred, I worked for them in my time as did brother George). We have already heard about the baker and then there was Bill Tompkins. It was Bill the Greengrocer who gave me my first taste of the entrepreneurial world. I don't recall how I got the job but I started working for Bill soon after his employers changed from the horse and cart to a van (though I do remember the horse relieving itself at one end as it chomped happily from its nosebag at the other!). The van was a foreign vehicle, I think, yellow in colour, with those slide down sides and back. God only knows what the weights and measures and health and safety people would make of it these days! Bill was on the road, on different 'rounds' six days out of seven, he kept a milk bottle behind his driving seat to piddle in, I can (if required, but don't ask), still describe the stench in the cab. To be sure, we had scales but we were just a little short of weights so if a customer asked for a quarter of mushrooms, we used a packet of tea! I just loved it. To start with I worked only on Saturdays, later (as I became more astute), I took every opportunity to work with Bill. On a Saturday I met Bill at the bottom of Links Way at around nine o'clock in the morning. He would delve deep into his leather cash bag (I always wanted one of those) and give me a handful of silver coins, a handful of copper coins and two ten shilling notes, this was my change for the day. Boy did I work, I loved knocking on the doors, taking the orders and weighing up the green grocery and other items we had on board. Bill's son Pete, helped his dad and I didn't figure out at first just why we needed as many helpers, I did later! It didn't take me long to realise that, if Bill didn't count the change he gave at the start of the day and didn't count the cash I returned to him at the end of it, he had little idea what I had taken at any given time! What joy, what bliss, what status! By this time and for some unknown reason, I was at a Grammar School, how I hated it, all those 'posh' people with funny accents, those teachers wearing stupid looking gowns and mortarboards. In truth I was frightened stiff, my mum was basking in working class glory, her son was at Grammar School, must take out some Provident Cheques to pay for the uniform, can't wait to tell everyone. The one saving grace was Bill the Greengrocer's inability to count the money at the end of Saturday. True, he paid me seven shillings and sixpence and true, I gave that to mum, but what I salted away was mine! And so I became very popular at school. I was the one who, when everyone else was eating school dinners, popped over the road to the café for egg and chips. I was also the one who, if Jennifer Norwood agreed to let me take her to the cinema, could afford to go upstairs! It all came to a sad end (for my mum at least). I had a friend who was older than me, he drove a laundry van for a living and I, believing that this would increase my earning power, 'bunked off school' to join him on his daily collections. It went well at first, Keith started to teach me to drive the van! I got a little ahead of myself and dumped the thing into a ditch. The next day was worse still, whistling away, I grabbed a box of laundry, noting the address, (not the name, big mistake!) I trundled up the garden path, knocked at the door and was greeted by an elderly gentleman whose face seemed somehow familiar. Colonel Goad was the chairman of the school governors, the following day he reported to my headmaster that a young fellow wearing our school blazer had delivered the colonel's laundry. My poor old mum was summoned to the inner sanctum and told that this was a stroke too far, the Head felt it was time to say farewell to JP! It was a Wednesday as I recall, by Friday I had a job at Burtons the Tailors. I had to tell Bill the Greengrocer that I was resigning!

My dad died when I was a Housemaster in an Approved School, I had got to know him very much better in his latter years. He often visited us when we were living in Suffolk; of my kids, only Sarah remembers him at all which is a shame. 'AG' loved gambling on the horses and the dogs, starred in a couple of films with Barbara Woodhouse (the dog lady) worked bloody hard all his life and never, ever gave up the fight. For me, the abiding memories of my dad are of a fighter, a man who, despite everything, provided for his family and enjoyed a laugh. I just wish that I could find a copy of the Watford Observer that tells the story of dad being arrested. He was on his way to his 'second' job of the day. As always he was riding his bike (purchased with money won on Vernons Pools) but a policeman happened to be standing by the traffic lights at the bottom of Baldwins Lane when 'AG' crossed on a red light. The headline ran, "Out of my Way Say's Cyclist" for goodness sake dad was on his way to work! No policeman in his right mind would have stopped him. Mum outlived the 'old man' by many years, I told you she was a fighter. One story sums up our mum. In my first book I related some stories about my childhood and mentioned a lad named Peter Priggen. Despite the fact that I told readers that Peter was a bit of a jerk, he contacted me and told me something about my mum I had never known. Pete's mum died (I think in childbirth) and my mum agreed with his dad, to care for Peter to enable his dad to continue working. Peter's dad was Austrian by birth and, when you bear in mind the times he was living in, things could not have been easy. Peter told me that he remembers my mum with a great deal of affection.

My mum had faults, we all have, but she knew how to hold a baby and stop it crying, she knew how to get you going when things were bad, she also knew how to chuck you under the table when the doodlebugs were raining down! If people were short of grub and Mrs 'P' had just one crust, she would make sure they shared it with her family. My mum was bloody useless at managing money, proud of her kids, fought every day of her life with my dad but never deserted him and he never deserted her, old fashioned? Maybe, silly and sloppy, probably, but I am here to prove that mum and dad stayed together despite their problems and there are a fair number of little Pilgrims out there who remember them with affection.

Wonderful memories, sad memories each and everyone of them priceless to the character of any family. I have tried to inspire you to have a go at your family history. Brother Bill fully intends to leave ours in the hands of all those other Pilgrims out there. Hopefully they will keep it going. Go on write it down!

The Little Shop by Kings Langley Station needs a 'blue plaque'! As J.P. and Spainy eat here!

SPAINY TELLS HIS STORY

So, Having Indulged Myself, I invited Mr Spain To Do The Same He thought about it, (his family history that is), rubbed his chin, hoisted his trousers to roughly where his waist should be, grunted, wiped away a stain from his tee shirt, adjusted his tripod, checked his telephoto lens, ensured that his fly buttons were done up and suggested a compromise. Here it is:

" John suggested that I tell my 'story' but I came to the conclusion that to give an account of an unexceptional, middle class upbringing living in Radlett and Watford in Hertfordshire, and Melbourne in Australia during my childhood, as well as going to Preparatory and Public Schools (where, unlike John, I enjoyed my schooldays), would send everyone to sleep.

Here I have to intervene, for the above you should read: "I am far too modest to suggest that my childhood was banal and boring or that I travelled across the world (therefore making me a far more interesting person than J.P.) or, indeed that some of those halcyon days were spent cavorting with wallabies and kangaroos! (don't ask!).

"Instead I will tell you about the time I went hunting for Morag the Monster! I was sent off in a private company jet from Luton Airport to Glasgow, where I drove myself **(no chauffeur 'Spainy'?)** to Mallaig, a fishing port on the west coast of Scotland. In those days I was an industrial photographer working for GEC Marconi. I had been given a secondment to photograph on Loch Morar, the largest freshwater Loch in Scotland on behalf of a research team from London University, who were testing out GEC Marconi Sonar equipment **(at this point in the story Mr Spain explains what 'Sonar' is for my benefit, I didn't need his explanation, I've watched Hans and Lotte Hass!).** "The research team's mission was to find anything unusual in the Loch as there had been unsubstantiated sightings of several large creatures **(even more sightings when Spainy arrived on the scene!).** One must bear in mind that this Loch is not accessible from the sea therefore the notion of a monster was even more intriguing. During one of our forays out onto the Loch looking for what the locals call 'Morag the Monster', (which seemed to get larger and more ferocious depending on which pub one was in and the time of day you happened to be there!), the Army turned up unannounced for manoeuvres on the Loch, making it impossible for us to carry out any tests. The captain in charge of the army operation **(wait for it!)** turned out to be a boy I was at school with! **(Well I never! Do tell us more David).** He immediately assigned a 'squaddie' to carry my photographic equipment **(see what I mean?),** and I was invited to photograph the army exercise (having obtained clearance) from a helicopter. I enjoyed the experience **(I guess you did, since some poor 'squaddie' had to carry the equipment!)** and I dined with the officers as well! When the army had gone I went back to the search for 'Morag' with the research team who had gone sightseeing while the army was there. A few days later while snoozing at the front of the boat **(That's the sharp end 'Spainy', commonly known as the bow!),** on a quiet evening with the sunset and the mists beginning to appear on the still Loch, there was a shout, 'David get round here!' As it happens I wasn't as large then as I am now, in fact I was fit and trim **(sez you).** I rushed to the makeshift sonar cabin (on the equally makeshift boat) to be shown the screen, on which there were three blips or echoes (to use the correct terminology).   One of the research scientists pointed excitedly at the screen and said " Daddy, Mummy and baby" referring to the randomly moving blips of three supposed 'Morags'. I never found out whether this was true as we never got a visual sighting, but just what were those blips?"

Typical of Spainy, use the lower classes to carry your equipment for a few days, dine with the officers, then feed us a load of old codswallop about monsters! He explained

to me that, maybe everyone has been looking in the wrong place for monsters. He suggests that they should have been looking in Loch Morar, not Loch Ness. It is difficult to understand his logic, since they found nothing in either Loch!

CHAPTER 11 - THE EXPERTS

'Cuddly' Ken Thomson - Veterinary on BBC Three Counties Radio

Every Wednesday afternoon 'Cuddly' arrives at the studios, usually he is in a rush and so he hasn't had time to take off the green 'wellies' and long gloves! Ken is our 'vet' and a better man for the job you will never meet. His knowledge is second to none, true, not all of it is of a veterinary nature! Quite simply, for me as a broadcaster, Ken is a gift, blessed with a wonderful sense of humour and years of experience. Mr Thomson is beloved by my listeners, but enough of the old flannel, let Ken tell you about himself:

"I was born in a Derbyshire village in the year of our lord 1946, thus I am younger than Mr Pilgrim and it shows! Most of the villagers were related so that explains a lot as well! It was impossible to be naughty because you could be certain that someone would tell your dad, or maybe just cuff you around the ear! So it was that even when I had been at my most angelic, I would return home to another bout of concussion administered by father! I had many pets, from the usual cats and dogs to a mouse that my mother would not allow into the house. I shared the cost of caring for the mouse with a younger and more impressionable cousin who I allowed to own the front of this female rodent, whilst I owned the rear. My reason for negotiating this financial deal was quite simple. Any offspring would arrive at my end of the arrangement thus enabling me to capitalise on the investment! Sadly it was not be, my brother announced that the mouse was, in fact a male. This discovery ensured two things for my future. Any money making schemes would be sure to founder and I would become a vet in order to avoid such humiliation in the future.

Secondary School was Buxton College until my GCE's (I got eight) then I followed my parents, who had moved to Wales (probably in a desperate bid to avoid me) and I attained three A levels at Grammar School in Caernafon. I decided to go to Liverpool University to study Vet Science and in order to enjoy the Beatles backlash and to be close enough to home never to have to do my own washing. Yet again my cunning ploy failed, the closest I came to the Beatles was a feeling of having eight legs to cope with on a Saturday night after a particularly strong shandy and mum refused to do any laundry stating that it was 'character forming'.

It was too late to change and so, after five years I qualified as a vet and took up my first job as a small animal assistant in St Helen's, Lancashire. This was a steep learning curve in a young vets development and in no time I acquired a taste for black puddings and travel. Thus it was that I decided to move, ignoring my grandmother's advice never to trust anyone south of Sparrowpit (there's one for Mr Pilgrims cryptic out and about questions). I moved south, first to London, then to Luton where I have stayed ever since. I love my profession and I have never regretted becoming a vet, I only trust that my clients especially my patients feel the same way!"

Out and About with 'Cuddly' Ken Thomson!

BEHAVE YOURSELVES! VIC BOTTERILL-EX POLICEMAN, NOW A PUBLIC SPEAKER

Vic Botterill was born in a castle at Matlock, Derbyshire, he wasn't an aristocrat or even a nobleman though! Here's Vic's explanation: *"My mother was evacuated from London to Matlock and the castle had been transformed into a maternity unit for the duration of the war. My mum was widowed two years later and I was passed from relative to relative and eventually ended up in an orphanage. Eventually Mrs Botterill remarried and I settled in Oxhey near Watford. I passed my eleven plus exams and went to Rickmansworth Grammar School. I can't say this was a wonderful experience because I wasn't any good at exams. This was partly because of the onset of puberty which made girls more interesting than the exams. I was caned twice for altering or wearing my school uniform in such a way as to "bring the school into disrepute," in my view my*

alterations made me more attractive to the opposite sex, I cringe now at the very thought of how I must have looked. It was while I was at school that I met a certain Mr J. Pilgrim. Here was another individual who was not going to be pushed around by the system. The funny thing is that we both finished up working for organisations which had strict hierarchical management structures! I didn't do well at the exams (a grammar school failure, now known as a late developer) I bummed around various jobs, until I eventually joined the police at the age of twenty one. A year later I married Shirley. I spent eight years of service trying to pass my sergeants exam, passed and then spent a further twelve years trying to pass the Inspectors Exam. By this time I had discovered the secrets of study and passed with more than 80%. I base part of my talk called "Moments, Memories and Magic" on this experience. I then obtained a degree grounded in Philosophy and the police promoted me to Chief Inspector. For about fifteen years I was involved in training Law and Procedure and went on to deal with human behaviour, ranging from management, communication, interviewing, memory, stress, race relations and equal opportunities.

About half way through my thirty years of service, when I was a sergeant at Hertford, I was called upon to escort a couple of 'naughty lads' back to an Approved School just outside the town. Expecting to be met by some sort of soft headed liberal attempting to control some of the little horrors, I was surprised to hear a familiar voice berating the little darlings! It was John Pilgrim. We exchanged memories and agreed to get together some time. John may have worked for Social Services and was obviously very successful because his charges thought the world of him, respected his integrity and responded well to his discipline. His ready sense of humour, disrespect for unthinking, unearned authority is something he has undoubtedly retained to this day.

It was eighteen years later that John, having seen an article in an entertainment magazine concerning a professional speaker doing the rounds called Vic Botterill, he said "I saw the name and thought there can only be one person called that, am I right?" He was and I have been a regular contributor to John's 'Out and About' programme ever since."

I was well pleased to meet up with Vic again, he is a great bloke, even if he was a copper for thirty years! **Call Vic on 01992 500922 or visit his website www.afterdinnerspeaker.co.uk**

A young PC Vic Botterill

CHARLIE ROSS.

Charlie is our antiques expert on the 'Out and About' programme, like our other experts he is so knowledgeable it would be easy to dislike him! but you simply can't because, again like our other experts, he loves his subject and still gets excited about it. Here's Charlie's description of himself:

"I was born in Aylesbury, Bucks in 1950, spent 1957 to 1967 in prison (Berkhamsted School actually, it just felt like prison). I left school with reasonable cricketing and long jumping skills but little in the way of academic qualifications. I joined the W.S. Johnson company, a local firm of chartered surveyors; they had an auction room in Buckingham. I worked under the expert guidance of John Collings and (with no warning) was soon placed on the auctioneers rostrum! I sold my first ever lot to a stroppy ex-military type for less than the reserve price, good way to start or what? Never did it again! In 1973 I became self employed and worked as a freelance auctioneer, dealer, dabbler etc. before starting the firm Donner-Ross (with Alan Donner) in 1983. We moved to Woburn soon after forming the company. Donner Ross became Douglas Ross in 1999 after a merger with Downer-Duff of Milton Keynes."

Charlie lists some other memories:

"Selling veteran and vintage cars in Alexandra Palace (before it burned down!). Finding a Fantin Latour (French impressionist) in a brown paper bag in the vaults of a Nat West Bank, it subsequently sold for £200, 000. Selling a Georgian cupboard in Woburn for £66,000. Playing Henry Higgins in My Fair Lady at the Playhouse Theatre, Oxford. Conducting numerous charity auctions up and down the country, including the Grand Prix Ball at Silverstone. Once selling a self portrait of Frank Bruno!" That's Charlie Ross!

Phone 01525 290502 for the showrooms.

Charlie Ross, antiques expert on the Out and About programme

"Phil's in Pinner"

Alittle over a year ago a new listener and caller joined our happy band. It was obvious from the start that Phil had a lot to say on a wide and varied array of topics. Soon he became one of our regular experts, joining me in the studio to advise listeners on jewellery, watches, gemstones etc. It didn't end there! We got to discussing astronomy one afternoon and it turned out that, not only was Phil something of an expert himself, but he knows the one and only Sir Patrick Moore! We chatted to Sir Patrick at his home in Sussex and he kindly invited us to visit him to make a programme, I'm looking forward to that. Oh yes and then there is Bonsai! Phil knows a bit about that as well and then there is music and then....well let him tell you about himself.

"In 1971 a small, blond boy left his school in Harrow for the last time, no not THE Harrow but Lascelles Secondary Modern no less. Clutching his grade four CSE, pottery result he scuttled off to the then, Youth Employment Agency and somehow ended up with an apprenticeship in goldsmithing, sitting at the feet of the craftsmen from Garrards and Aspreys. After making tea for five years he eventually gained his articles (better late than never!). Only then did his father admit that, upon first hearing of his son's chosen profession that he had left the room to actually fall on the floor and roll about in hysterical laughter at the thought of his hamfisted son becoming a jeweller!"

'Phil's motto is 'always walk the path less travelled and if anything is worth doing, it's worth overdoing'.

Whilst living in a tiny village in remote, rural West Wales a tatty violin was thrust into his hands and a new hobby was born. This eventually became a small business named, tongue in cheek, Driftwood Strings where nearly two hundred violins have been restored and sold, one to an old flame of Nigel Kennedy and Phil got to play an Irish jig on a Stradivarius worth a cool seventy five thousand pounds! For a while Phil had Prince Charles own cello in his house, made originally for James I, it was also played by a top cellist in Phil's front room, not bad for a daft hobby.

Apart from a dozen guitars (Phil has played guitar since he was ten years old) there is a small forest of sixteen Bonsai trees that ensure he gets out of the workshop sometimes, to water them! Then there are the telescopes, Phil's longest passion has been for astronomy , his old dad, on seeing a garden filled with home made telescopes pointing heavenward once remarked "When are the bloomin Heinkels due over then? It looks like an ack - ack gunners convention." Most of his teenage years were spent in the garden gazing at heavenly bodies to the wee small hours and this probably explains why he eventually became the well balanced person he is today!

Once, after a fairly average day which had seen Phil trying to convince the property buyer from Pinewood Studios (who had called in for some bits of jewellery for the new Bond movie) to buy his wreck of a Lada car for Mr Brosnan to drive in Red Square rather than that boring Aston Martin. Brosnan will never know what he missed! Later the same day there was a knock at the door, three Russians stood on the doorstep (in response to a free add in the local newspaper). One of these unshaven, leather coated giants muttered "Ve haff kum vor ze LADA." As we strolled towards said vehicle, Phil tried the only bit of Russian he knew (salvaged from a BBC record) and the response was dramatic! "The tugboat captain on the Volga always keeps his hand firmly on the tiller," has that effect you know! Assuming that Phil must be a member of the Pinner Branch of the Russian Mafia, they asked if he had any more Ladas, Phil muttered "Sorry, just the one" and dashed indoors counting his money and thinking to himself "Hmmm another hobby." Then, in a rare moment of common sense, Phil decided to end the afternoon doing something sensible, "Hmmm, I know, how about phoning a radio show, some bloke called Pilgrim, you can't get into any scrapes doing that can you? anything for a quiet life."

On a serious note… my dad died a few weeks before his first grandson was born. I can still hear him now, twenty years on, singing Clive Dunn's song 'Granddad'. Every time the song 'The Living Years' by Mike and the Mechanics is on the radio, I still choke up. Both my dad and granddad (also a passionate astronomer) died at fifty. I've only got four years to go and hope to break the family tradition hence the passions. As grandma said, "You've got forever pushing up the daisies, but only seventy or eighty years to pick them, so pick as many as you can and make the most of them."

Phil with Sir Patrick Moore

Phil admiring Sir Patrick's telescope

ALAN GOLDSMITH - THE HOUSE ON THE HILL TOY MUSEUM AND A CASTLE!

Sometime when he and I are not busy (which probably means it will never happen) I must find out more about Alan Goldsmith! I know that during the sixties Alan promoted rock and roll concerts, I know that he has worked with just about anyone who is anyone in show business, I know that he still promotes concerts and I know that he runs the House on the Hill Toy Museum and that he built a castle! Whenever Alan comes into the studios as our toy expert the telephone lines run hot. It seems that the world and his brother have something or other in their loft or in the garage that they saved from their childhood. I have never known Mr Goldsmith not to have knowledge of any toy any caller mentions, he knows his business inside out. The history of toys is a fascinating subject! We will get to the castle later!

It's the largest privately owned Toy Museum in Europe with over 30,000 items on display. Ranging from the late Victorian era through to the eighties, the collection is based on the 'Hornby' train set owned by one man who began collecting in 1946 using his pocket money. The House on the Hill opened its doors in 1991 and despite the comprehensive collection the museum is always interested in purchasing toys of interest.

So let us begin a 'brief encounter' with toys. Children's Annuals have been published for more than one hundred and fifty years. I still recall the sheer joy of opening my Rupert or Eagle Annual when I was kid, they were (and still are) my favourites but there are many more. Collecting has gone on for years but it began in earnest in the late nineteenth century when publishers of 'Boys Own', 'Chums', and 'Chatterbox' stockpiled each issue and produced an 'annual' at Christmas. First editions of annuals can fetch high prices. Titles such as the Beano and Dandy are fetching higher prices than some of their predecessors mainly because people who read those comics as a kid want to re live their childhood, and who doesn't, except of course for David Spain, who hasn't come out of his first childhood yet. Prior to the Second World War titles such as Billy Bunter, Chips, Sexton Blake, Radio Fun, Butterfly, Jester, Tip Top, Sparkler, Crackers, Bubbles, Rainbow, Tiger Tim and the Holiday Annual still attract the collectors eye. The end of the Second World War saw an amazing increase in the manufacture of children's toys and annuals. Throughout the 1950's and 60's Television programmes added a new dimension to toys and books. Roy Rogers, Buffalo Bill, Bonanza, Champion the Wonder Horse, Rin Tin Tin, Lone Ranger and Hopalong Cassidy, all these names conjur up memories of our childhood. Space Annuals started with the Eagle, these books catered for the boys but the girls had their favourites as well. Girl's Own, Beryl the Peril, Schoolgirl, Crystal, Twinkle, Mandy, Girl's Fun, Princess are just some of the titles the ladies may remember with affection. 'Spainy informs me that Bunty was also popular with the girls, quite how he knows this I'm not sure! Take a look in your attic or your garage and don't, I repeat DO NOT THROW YOUR OLD ANNUALS AWAY UNTIL YOU HAVE THEM VALUED.

As we ambled around the toy museum 'Spainy' and I became strangely 'at one', we began discussing our child-hoods, true they were somewhat different in many ways, but similar in others. We both recalled many happy hours playing with board games. "Roman soldiers played board games on Hadrians Wall you know." I raised my eyebrows before asking, " Really, what did they play, Monopoly?" "I don't think so, why should they have played Monopoly?" "Well they had just about conquered everywhere in Europe." He chose to ignore my little quip and continued with his potted history of board games. "In the last hundred and fifty years loads of board games and other games have come and gone, some though are still popular, tiddlywinks, marbles, card games, hoops, shooting and skittle games. Other games are based on TV and radio programmes, 'Dad's Army,' 'Eamonn Andrews Quiz Game,' and 'Twenty Questions'," he continued. He seemed to be enjoying himself relating this information, so I left him to it. While 'Spainy' mused I moved on to take a look at some 'Barbies'.

Barbie was born in 1959 and she remains one of the world's best loved and most well known dolls; over seven hundred million Barbie dolls have been sold world-wide! The accessories alone must have netted the manufacturers a fortune - Barbie has her own cars, house, a horse, swimming pool and naturally her own boyfriend, Ken. Ken appeared in 1965, personally I was never sure about Ken but maybe that's just the way I am. Hundreds of different outfits have been produced for Barbie e.g. night-wear, ball-gowns, swimsuits you name it Barbie has it in her wardrobe. She is still as popular today as she ever was, despite the fact she has been going for over forty years and wasn't exactly a baby when she started! Maybe, in the future, you will be able to purchase a bit of plastic surgery for your Barbie! It's only my view of course but Ken required a facelift when he first came out (Came out?). Anyway, having had a word with Barbie I wandered back to find my photographer friend who hadn't noticed that I had left. "The most popular and enduring of all board games are Monopoly, Ludo, Scrabble and Cluedo they have all been enjoyed by five generations." He turned to look at me through hooded eyes, "I hope that you have been paying attention," "Oh yes, very interesting what about 'Kerplunk' and 'Buckaroo' then?" "Yes they are popular as well, and collecting board games is also becoming very popular."

REMEMBER! DON'T THROW THEM AWAY BEFORE YOU HAVE THEM VALUED.

Having experienced my friend's discourse on board games, I decided that we should move on and ask Alan Goldsmith himself to tell us about dolls. "Dolls" I said, "Well" said 'Spainy', "There was this girl in Brazil, did you know that some of them have blue eyes, it's something to do with Scottish and German origins." "Not that sort of doll, you plonker, children's dolls", "Ah, yes" he said losing interest. So here is Mr Goldsmith on the subject of dolls:

"Man has made images of his own likeness for well over a thousand years, so it is impossible to tell the complete story of dolls. Ancient civilisations fashioned dolls from cheap and available materials, such as rags, stone, wood and animal hides. Some very early examples of Peruvian and Egypto-Roman dolls have been found in graves, buried alongside their young owners. It seems that commercial production of wooden dolls in England began in the 16th century, German and Italian dolls were produced a little later. By the early 19th century, English wooden dolls were losing their appeal in favour of principally Austrian peg dolls, known as 'Grodnertals'. Queen Victoria owned one of the best known collections of these dolls. The early mid- eighteen hundreds saw several improvements in the design and manufacture of dolls. Mortschmann introduced the 'baby doll' but prior to this dolls had taken the form of miniature women, or sometimes men. The fabric doll industry thrived between 1900 and 1930 when realistic dolls were produced in Germany. 'Bisque' is an often heard word in the world of dolls. It simply means a fired clay with no finishing glaze, two principal manufacturers of 'bisque' dolls were France and Germany, companies such as Bru, Jumeau, Simon and Halbig, Armand Marseille, Kammer and Reinbdhart being among the most well known. In the 18th and 19th centuries good quality - life like dolls were often made from solid wax and had human hair, sold to toy-makers by the general public to make a bit of extra money."

Interior of the Toy Museum, a journey back into childhood memories

There is so much to take in at the Toy Museum, 'Spainy', having moved on from board games - he has always been partial to the odd game of Ludo, discovered next the farm toys! How well I remember my first farmyard! I was still at Primary School, well to be perfectly accurate, school was St. Oswald's church, Croxley Green, it was just after the war and proper schools were still being built. I had to stand up in front of the school to show everyone what I received for my birthday. Looking back it was a bloody silly thing for the teachers to do, after all how could they know whether a kid had got much for their birthday or not. Still it was with great pride that I showed off my lead farmyard! At The Toy Museum you will find a veritable treasure chest of farmyard memorabilia. 'Spainy' had little idea of what he was looking at because, as a public schoolboy he spent his youth thinking that milk came from bottles and had no idea at all that a cow was responsible. The most prominent manufacturer of farm toys, animals, machinery and related items was the Company, Richard Britain. They produced a huge variety of lead items including livestock, carts, trees, machinery and figures, in fact the company branched out into military items as well. With the success of Britain's other companies became involved in the toy farm market - with names such as Crescent, John Hill and Co., Charbens, Timpo, Salco, Taylor and Barnett and Wendall producing agricultural items, none were quite as successful as Britain's. The 'Britain' Company employed home workers who were paid, per figure, to paint the items. Some rarities produced at the time included the village idiot, a Jersey cow with a bell and a dairy cow with a map of the world painted over her! The company switched from lead to plastic when it was discovered that lead was toxic. Lead toys are highly collectable today, many of them can be seen at the Toy Museum.

MOUNTFITCHET CASTLE

At the outset I informed you that, as well as owning the House on the Hill Toy Museum, Alan Goldsmith had built a castle, I wasn't joking. Mountfitchet Castle is a national Historic Monument, protected by the Department of the Environment (as, indeed is David Spain). It is believed to have been an early Iron Age fort and Roman, Saxon and Viking settlements. Artefacts found on the site support this belief. In 1066, the site was attacked by the Normans and Robert Gernon, the Duke of Boulogne, built his castle here, making it his chief seat and the head of his Barony. It is said that Gernon was related directly to William the Conqueror. The male line of the Gernon family continued for five generations. The time of Robert Gernon's death is not known but William, his son and heir dropped the name Gernon and took the name Mountfitchet. In 1203, William died leaving his son Richard a minor, who became a royal ward of King John and was placed in the care of one Roger de Lacey, Constable of Chester. As soon as he came of age, Richard de Montfitchet appears to have joined the Baronial opposition to the King, his reasons are obscure, but oppose King John he did. John was swift with his reprisals and it seems that Mountfitchet was among the castles to be destroyed. After the attack by King John, the villagers took the stones to build houses and the castle site lay overgrown and forgotten for over seven hundred years! Enter one Alan Goldsmith! He has re-built Mountfitchet and it stands there today for all to see. The kitchens reveal what it would have been like over seven hundred years ago to produce a meal for the high and mighty. A selection of wild game, fish and vegetables is on display, much of the food would have been served on stale bread, used as platters. The garden would have been well stocked with herbs and vegetables used both for food and to supply the alchemist with items for his medicinal cures.

The entrance to Mountfitchet Castle

The Catapult or mangonel was based on a Roman design which the Normans copied and used for nearly a century after the Conquest, the carved heads on the front of the catapult are to frighten the attacking armies.

We know from the Domesday records that as well as a church at the castle, there was also a resident priest. This suggests that the castle was a place of some significance. The priest would have been the only literate member of the castle community. The construction of the Church is from oak beams made into planks for the walls, with a reed roof. You will see the intricate carvings around the doorway depicting the Tree of Life and Christ in Majesty.

The gallows were used for hanging miscreants and perpetrators of more serious crimes, victims were made to stand on a cart which was then drawn away leaving them to hang. The bodies would have been hung on the gallows for a period of time, as a warning to others. So the old rocker Alan Goldsmith, toy expert extraordinary built a castle! He's a great bloke, good friend and a right good story teller as well.

To see the Toy Museum and View the Castle, telephone: 01279 813237

CHAPTER 12 - THE ODD 'CELEB' OR THREE OR FOUR

It's inevitable, when you have a day job like mine, you are going to get to meet and speak with well known people. Some are well aware of their celebrity status some are not, some make you well aware of their celebrity status, others enjoy it but handle it. Some years ago I visited the Theatre Royal, Bath, it was close to Christmas and the theatre was well into it's annual pantomime season. I knocked at the stage door and made myself known, suitably reassured and with an air of self importance, the stage door keeper directed me to the dressing room of a lady who, up until that moment, I knew as 'Dot Cotton' in Eastenders. June Brown's voice answered my knock at the door, I entered, there she was in all her splendour! Two male fans who came from the Isle of Wight were with her, she dismissed them with a regal air, "I'm sorry lads I have to do an interview for BBC Radio." Fans gone, June invited me to sit down, she was dressed in her panto costume and heavily made up ready for the evening performance. We chatted, I begged a cigarette from her (not often I find myself without a packet of ciggies, but I did that afternoon). June gave me a full packet "Help yourself dear, I get them cheap, because 'Dot' smokes I think." They were mentholated, which I hate, but devils can't be choosers and anyway June offered me a glass of Sherry as well. About an hour and a half later I stumbled from the dressing room in love with June Brown. What a nice lady, generous with the Sherry as well! Totally without 'side' June carried out the interview as professionally as you would expect. She loves donkeys, would you believe? Even recorded a record in aid of a donkey sanctuary. I blundered across the stage of the Theatre Royal and bumped into an elderly gentleman wearing a duffle coat and peaked cap, "Sorry" I said "No bother," said Buster Merryfield, "Which way is the stage door?" Buster got into the acting game late in life and relished every moment, I was pleased to have bumped into him! Quiet, unassuming and a little shy, that is how I would describe Kevin Whately, star of 'Auf Wiedersehen Pet', 'Morse' and several other great TV programmes. Kevin was opening a charity event at Waddesden Manor when we met. He looked as if he felt a bit out of place when he arrived so I waited for a lull in the conversation and approached him, I was well aware that, even though you have an interview booked at 'gigs' like this, you have to be a bit pushy in order that the 'opposition' don't get in first. I suggested that we take a walk outside to tape the interview, stating that I wanted a breath of air, Kevin readily agreed and we walked towards the splendid aviary they have at Waddesden.

Candidly Kevin informed that he wanted to be a doctor when he was younger and that he didn't really think that acting was an important job, "after all, doctors do so much more good don't they?" I completed the interview and left annoyed with myself for not setting up another, longer chat with Mr Whately, I rather think that there is a lot more to this pleasant and modest man. There is a great deal to Fatima Whitbread! She signed the box containing the tape of our interview with a kiss and an entreaty to 'Go For it John'. I liked Fatima the moment I walked into her office in Luton where she was working for a charity. Fatima Whitbread had a tough upbringing in children's homes and she has never forgotten her roots. Proud of her achievements, rightly so, proud of her adoptive parents and proud that they are proud.

Gloria Hunniford is glamorous and highly personable. We met first over the telephone, I forget the subject of the interview but I do remember her telling me that, as a child she always wanted to be Doris Day! "Funny that Gloria," I informed her, "I always wanted to marry Doris Day." We got on like a house on fire and ended up singing (live on air for the one and only time folks) 'The Deadwood Stage' from 'Calamity Jane.' A year later I was broadcasting from the Chelsea Flower Show, we had been on air for about an hour when I felt a tap on my shoulder, I turned around and there was Gloria! "Excuse me can you tell me where BBC television is?" she asked. "Gloria" I said, offering my hand, she smiled as only Gloria Hunniford can, took my hand and shook it "How nice to see you again." I informed her that I was surprised because we had never met before, and went on to explain about the 'Deadwood Stage" she smiled that smile again "John" (she remembered!) "It's you, you old flirt!" Made my day you did Gloria!

Roy Hudd is, quite simply one of my favourite comedians and actors, so much so, that when I was offered the chance to interview him I turned it down. Asked why, I explained that there are some people who you admire so much that you don't want to be disillusioned. I remained firm in my decision until I heard the name Laurie Bellew mentioned on the telephone, my BA at Three Counties Radio was still trying to organise the Hudd interview and told me that Laurie would organise it! Mr Bellew was a man I had met just once, some three years before in London. I forget exactly which radio or TV idea I was peddling at the time, but Laurie had been kind enough to see me, buy me lunch and encourage me. He was the man who gave that great broadcaster John Dunn, so much encouragement at the start of his career. Laurie had also been a personal friend of James Stewart one of my all time heroes. In fact (given that I had refused to interview Roy Hudd) it was a strange link. I had managed to contact Laurie about a possible interview with Stewart (don't ask me how) and it was he who told me that the actor was unwell, had been in fact, ever since the death of his dear wife. Laurie had promised to contact Stewart but I had declined, saying that I wanted to remember the great man as he once was, and had no wish to impose on his personal grief. Anyway, back to Roy Hudd, Mr Bellew greeted me over the telephone like a long lost brother, "Pilgrim you old bugger what are you doing now, you owe me a meal." I explained my dilemma concerning Mr Hudd. "You fool, Roy is a great bloke, just as you imagine him to be, don't worry he won't explode your vision." I interviewed Roy, he was a real gent, the only comedian I have ever interviewed who didn't mind sharing the gags and the laughter, what a pro! He even informed that Laurie owed him several meals as well!

I'm not exactly sure that the next three characters should be included in my 'celebs' category, they are politicians! Anyway, one morning I waltzed into the reception area of Three Counties Radio and there, waiting to do an interview were, not in any particular order, you understand, William Hague, Michael Portillo and Sebastian Coe. Pilgrim couldn't allow the chance to pass, so I dashed off to find a copy of my first book , dashed back and asked them to sign it so that I could raffle it for a good cause. Portillo muttered something about Pilgrim being a good name for someone who got Out and About, Hague got Portillo to guide his hand across the page (only joking William) and Coe managed to stop pacing up and down as he spoke on his mobile phone long enough to sign (it could have been a blank cheque as far as Mr Coe was concerned, I missed out there). The real impression I was left with following that political encounter was, the lack of presence, when you are in the company of such people you expect to feel some sort of charisma and there just wasn't any. I'm not making a political point just telling what I felt. Oh yes, as I was leaving Hague asked me which good cause the book would be raffled for. "The Luton Labour Party" I cheekily replied.

Paul Daniels magician, conjurer, entertainer was completely different. I began our interview fully prepared to have a bit of a go at him. At the time Paul was not appearing on television, he was promoting his wife Debbie and her tour. I felt that Paul was a bit pathetic really and that he was being used. I ended the interview feeling that this was a man who really wanted his wife to succeed, yes, he did believe that he had been let down by people in the profession, but still had a point to make. Later on my mate Ernie Almond told me that he had met Paul on several occasions, at various Magic Circle meetings and Paul always helped out with setting up the chairs and all that bit, never used the fact that he was a big star, I know Ernie well and accept what he told me. Following our interview I watched a documentary on TV showing Paul and Debbie on tour, Paul was back on the road to finance Debbie's tour I still feel that Paul Daniels has missed out, but respect him for what he has done to support his wife.

Larry Adler! Now there was a man who did almost everything, seen most everything and, most certainly had an opinion on everything! I decided that I must, simply must interview Adler after hearing him on another radio station. Larry used to telephone talk radio stations a lot with his opinions on just about everything. Sometimes, if you caught him at the wrong moment Larry could cut you off, always he was a genuine, honest and very talented human being. We talked the first time about his compact disc 'The Glory of Gerswhin' which turned out to be a winner all over the world. Then we talked about his early life, Larry met Al Capone and George and Ira Gerswhin. In fact when he heard a youthful Larry Adler play his "Rhapsody in Blue", George stated "the goddamned thing sounds as though I wrote it for you." Jerome Kern, Cole Porter, Rodgers and Hart, the list of great and talented people Larry Adler had known is endless. I could have sat and listened to Larry talk for hours, he wasn't a name dropper, he simply loved to talk about people, places and events till the cows came home. Adler was born in Baltimore, he was thrown out of the Peabody Conservatory of Music for playing "Yes We Have No Bananas" instead of a piece by Grieg! Having run away to New York young Adler got his chance when Rudy Vallee put him on at his club. It seems unbelievable that one man crammed so much into one life, a game of tennis with the likes of Greta Garbo and Salvador Dali is just one of the stories he told me. Larry fell in love with Ingrid Bergman, they had an affair, but one of his most delightful memories was of playing "Rhapsody in Blue" in the Nuremberg stadium, a good Jewish boy playing in the place where Herr Hitler held his rallies! Sadly, just three weeks after I last spoke to him, Larry Adler passed away, he will always be remembered as a 'One off', what a man! God bless you Larry Adler.

Elkie Brookes is a great singer, she learned the art singing at her uncle Nat's Jewish get togethers. When we talked on the radio I introduced her as Elsie Brookes! "Did you call me Elsie?" Thinking quickly I answered, "No, but I will if you like?" She laughed and agreed, so I called her Elsie all through the interview.

And then of course the greatest celebrity I have ever met! Jon Gaunt! What! You've never heard of him! Well, if you haven't, you soon will. 'Gauntie' as he is known to his friends and listeners alike arrived at the radio station about four years ago. I was at home when his first show was broadcast and so I tuned in to listen to the man who was going to be a big star, I thought he was bloody awful! He has improved a bit since, winning three Sony Gold Radio Awards in one year, he's the first person ever to achieve that. He is brash, opinionated and passionate, at least that's what he tells me. Love him or hate him, you can't ignore my mate 'Gauntie'. He stayed at my house one night, we took off to the pub for a few drinks then sat in my lounge for a night cap (or two or three) 'Gauntie' went off to bed and so did I. At about three in the morning I had a 'call of nature'. I stumbled out of my bedroom and along the landing, looked up to see a naked 'Gauntie' disappearing into his bedroom! "Don't' say a word Pilgrim," he muttered. "I'm not saying anything, I'm off to buy a bike." "Oh yeah why is that then?" "I've just seen somewhere I can park it!" I accompanied Jon on a theatre tour recently, along with our mate Ernie Almond and we, all three, got to share dressing rooms. Ernie's involvement required him to appear in the first half of the show dressed as a radio anorak, one of 'Gaunties' faithful followers and 'Ern takes his work seriously. Each night he would dress up in trousers too short for him, plimsolls, a coloured shirt and tiny, rimless spectacles, yes I know it sounds sweet, but the really funny thing was to see Ernie pacing up and down, going through his lines dressed like that! On more than one occasion I was told to, "shut up telling jokes, I'm trying to remember my lines." To be honest he didn't actually use those words but you get the gist. I think that 'Jon Gaunt Live and Unleashed' was a bit of an eye opener for the listeners who came to see their hero. Sure some of the stories he told were very, very funny, but the other side of Jon Gaunt caught their imagination as well. He related tales of the bad times as well as the good, told how he made a lot (and I mean a lot) of money as a scriptwriter for television, appeared on TV in 'Boon' and 'Emmerdale Farm' etc. The tour was sell out success and a great experience. So much so, that we are off on the road again very soon. After my experience, when I made a 'call of nature', I advised 'Gauntie' that the title of the next tour should be 'Jon Gaunt Live and Undressed' but I don't think it will happen, but there again, you can never tell with Jon!

TELESCOPES AND SIR PATRICK MOORE

Astronomy came into my life in the shape of Phil from Pinner, whom we have already met, he says it's my fault, I say it's his and we both blame Sir Patrick Moore. Just how we got to talking about celestial bodies, I cannot recall, the 'Out and About' show is like that. Phil happened to mention that he had been inspired as lad, to purchase a telescope by watching and listening to Patrick Moore and the TV programme, 'The Sky at Night'. Aged sixteen, Phil made his way to Patrick's home in Selsey, Sussex. He stood at the gate of 'Farthings' and watched as, seemingly hundreds of people ambled in and out of the house. A man came up to him and asked what he was doing, Phil explained that he had hoped to meet Patrick Moore, he was invited in and left to wander at will. Patrick Moore's home is like that! So there you are then, Phil got in touch with the now, Sir Patrick, was invited to 'Farthings' again and then arranged for me to go with him to meet the great man. Phil drove and, as we approached the village of Selsey, he appeared to be becoming rather nervous, I asked him what was the matter? "I'm excited and nervous, you never know whether Patrick will remember that you are due to visit, he could be in a bad mood, who knows?" We parked opposite 'Farthings' and walked up the driveway, the first thing that struck me was the accessibility to the great man's garden. Small sheds, turrets etc. were dotted about the well kept lawn, some of them rather 'Heath Robinson' and probably reflecting the eccentric character of their designer! The house has a large porch and peering through the glass you can see a 1920's bicycle, the only cycle Patrick has ever owned, he rode it around the village until a couple of years ago. Tucked away in another corner there is the very first telescope Patrick purchased and a couple of globes of planets. On the door of the porch is a notice requesting all visitors to "Observe the Air Lock Precautions," this is designed to protect Patricks cat! By this time Phil's nervousness had got to me and I just wanted to turn around and go home, after all, I had never been particularly taken with Patrick Moore on television. I was aware of the esteem in which he is held in the world of space and astronomy naturally but to be perfectly honest, I was looking upon the visit as part of my job. A figure appeared at the door, Phil muttered a nervous greeting, Sir Patrick Moore invited us in and turned away leaving us to follow and to "Observe the air lock procedure". We dutifully followed Patrick along the hallway, he explained (over his shoulder) that he was about to carry out a telephone interview for Radio Five Live. We entered the study and were waved in the general direction of a couple of chairs, I placed a bottle of Irish whiskey (good advice from Phil!) on the table and Sir Patrick's eyes glinted, he gave a smile

and a 'thumbs up' sign, I looked at Phil, he smiled back, we were in!

Bearing in mind my earlier comments, you may be surprised at what I am about to tell you. Sir Patrick Moore is, without any doubt, the most generous, kind man it has ever been my privilege to meet. His enthusiasm is boundless, his knowledge faultless and his modesty genuine. "I am an amateur," he will tell you, "But amateurs have a lot to offer." Never a truer word, here is the man who has met and worked with all the great space pioneers, advised NASA on space travel, written over one hundred books, mapped the moon and other planets and appeared regularly on 'The Sky at Night' for forty five years, never missing a performance.

Eccentric? Possibly though eccentricity is, by its very nature, difficult to define. True the certificate proclaiming his recent Knighthood is nailed to the back of the study door! And true, the ribbon with the medal is framed alongside another small brass looking object. When I inquired what the object was, Patrick smiled an impish smile and informed me that he got it from a cereal packet some years ago and thought it went well in the frame! The study is a place you could investigate for hours, piles of books everywhere, a battered and rather old computer and the famous very, very old Underwood typewriter! The fireplace is reserved for cricket mementoes, photos of Patrick playing the game (he only stopped playing two years ago) cricket bats, cricket balls and other sporting memorabilia. If the Irish whiskey served its purpose my knowledge of cricket cemented our relationship. Sir Patrick Moore invited me into the lounge where we watched England playing Australia for the next three hours! Phil wandered off having been given the run of the house, Patrick is like that "Yes, yes go where you like, have you got a map of the moon, would you like one?" As we sat watching the television my eyes wandered as I took in the paraphernalia surrounding me. There was the legendary Xylophone (hand written notice above it "No, you may not place your empty glass on the Xylophone!"), a grand piano (Patrick began composing music at the age of ten), a photograph of his grandmother and of course, asleep on the best chair in the room, Patrick's beloved cat! Phil popped his head around the door, "Sir Patrick could I have a word with you please?" The great man left me watching TV and wondering what was going on, about fifteen minutes later the lounge door opened, Sir Patrick entered, wearing the famous monocle, he was carrying a tray with three small drinks on it, he offered Phil and myself the whiskey and took cold coffee for himself (medication makes it necessary to have 'non drinking days'). I was presented with a framed certificate proclaiming that I was now member of a very special society! So that was what they had been cooking up!

The International Society of the Fieldless was born on the island of Santorini in May 2000. It consists of a number of people who, whilst amongst a group of highly qualified scientists and astronauts attending the NASA 13th Symposium of Humans in Space considered themselves to be without a definite 'field'. The exception on the founding list being Sir Patrick Moore who cannot possibly be considered to be 'Fieldless', but insisted on being elected anyway! A very proud moment for me and typical of the generosity of Patrick Moore. So, it was back to the cricket until a sort of 'Professor' type turned up in the late afternoon, he had a special telescope with him so we all went into the garden to look at the sun, magnificent! Off then, for a tour of the various telescopes scattered in the shelters in the garden. The 'daddy' of them all is housed in what I can only describe as a cut down grain silo. The top half swivels by means of a 'Flash Gordon' type wheel! The telescope itself looks like something out of 'Buck Rogers in the 25th Century' but it was the one Phil wanted to get his hands on, later in the evening his wish would be granted. I mentioned that 'Farthings' is home from home for just about anyone who cares to turn up, and so it turned out when it came time to eat. Patrick gave us the choice, we could go to a local restaurant, he would cook something at home or we could order a 'Takeaway'. In any event, he intended to pay! Having agreed on the 'Takeaway', Professor type appeared with a choice of Indian, Chinese or Thai food and proceeded to act as waitress, taking our orders. About half an hour later, Phil and I were exploring the study again when a voice called, "It's getting cold!" We followed the chatter of voices to the dining room, where a couple of weeks before such monumental figures of history as Buzz Aldrin had dined. Professor and wife, their two children, Phil, Patrick and myself were joined by a gentleman who was staying with Patrick. After the meal the daylight had faded and it was decided that it was not going to be a good night to observe the stars, nevertheless we did stumble through the darkness to take a look at the big one! Patrick remained indoors, he was, by now a little tired. It was time for Phil to show off, he cranked the handle, opened a metal door and directed the telescope in the direction of Mars. Even though it was not a clear night, my first view of the heavens was simply wonderful. Sir Patrick is somewhat infirm these days and the most frustrating thing for him is that he is unable to operate his telescopes without assistance nor can he play his beloved Xylophone or the piano. It seems particularly cruel that these pleasures should be denied a man who has made the heavens, the stars and music his life. I fell asleep in the car on the way home, as I drifted off I reflected on a very special day and a very special man.

Sir Patrick Moore, a very special man, interviewed by J.P.

This book is dedicated to my brothers and sisters: June, Bill, George, Linda and Susan.

As the old saying goes, "You can choose your friends but you can't choose your family." I got really lucky when whoever it was chose my family for me. They have supported me through thick and thin, good times and bad. We have had our differences but remain loyal to one another, no family could ask for more, as for our mum and dad, if I never write another book (and believe me, I intend to), I cannot thank them enough for being, quite simply my mum and dad. As you will have read (and if you haven't, you skipped a page!), they often fought like 'cat and dog' but they stayed together to the end. Their kids still wish that they had got to know their mum and dad better, but I guess a lot of people would admit to that. If you believe in the hereafter, my mum and dad will be sitting on the same cloud arguing! He will be telling her that he will give her the top brick off the chimney and she won't believe him, God bless you both.

BIBLIOGRAPHY:

Curiosities of Bedfordshire - Pieter and Rita Boogart,   ISBN 1 857702166
S.B. Publications

Mad Lucas - Richard Whitmore,   ISBN 0902755021
North Herts District Council

The Buckinghamshire Book - Countryside Books   ISBN 0905392809

A Hertfordshire Valley - Scott Hastie and David Spain,   ISBN 0953863103
Published by Alpine Press

Bedfordshire - James Dyer   ISBN 0747802696
Shire County Books

The Book of Radlett and Aldenham - Donald Wratten   ISBN 086234649
WBC Books

The Northamptonshire Village Book,
Published by Countryside Books,
Newbury, Berkshire.

Leaflets and information guides from various Counties.

Please Note: Where I have quoted telephone numbers and opening times, they are correct at the time of printing.

If you have any difficulties please check your telephone book and don't ring me!

SAVE YOURSELF SOME MONEY!

The following venues have kindly agreed to some special offers.
Simply choose and **tear out the perforated token** from this book. Take it to the venue and they will do the rest.

Bedford Butterfly Park:
One adult free with one paying.
01234 772770

Buckinghamshire Railway Centre, Quainton:
For every adult paying, one child free.
01296 655450
(information line)

English School of Falconry:
One adult free with one paying.
01767 627527

Toy Museum & Mountfitchet
Castle: Visit both in one day 10%
discount. 01279 813237

The Cecil Higgins Gallery:
2nd ticket free with one full paying
adult. 01234 211222

Bekonscot Model Village:
one child free with one full
paying adult. 01494 672919

Woburn (Charlie Ross):
One item valued free.
01525 290502

Greensands Plant Centre:
10% Discount on every £10 spent.
01767 261461

Milton Earnest Garden Centre:
£1 deducted from each £5 spent.
01234 823033

Stondon Transport Museum:
One adult free with one paying.
01462 850339

Alan Dansey, computer expert

Have Your Family Page on the Out and About Website Free!

Our webmaster Alan Dansey will include a page about your family along with a couple of photographs free of charge! Telephone Alan for further details on **01767 310163** or contact the website:

www.outandabout.uk.net

Other books by John Pilgrim:

Out & About Book I
(published 1999)

Out & About Again Book II
(published 2000)

See pictures taken from David Spain's extensive photo archive and talk to John about people, places, memories, passions, gardening or what used to happen and what's happening now, on the 'Out & About' website.

John and David are also available for illustrated slide shows and talks. Please contact our website for details:

www.outandabout.uk.net

Some of the Staff at BBC Three Counties Radio, 2001

Mark Norman,
Managing Editor